Raise the Bottles

Huang Chun-Ming

Raise the Bottles

Translated from the Chinese
by Howard Goldblatt

BALESTIER PRESS
LONDON · SINGAPORE

Balestier Press
Centurion House, London TW18 4AX
1010 Dover Road #01-800, Singapore 139658
www.balestier.com

Raise the Bottles: Collected Stories
Copyright © Huang Chun-Ming, 1956—1971
English translation copyright ©Howard Goldblatt, 2021

The Gong from *The Taste of Apples*, by Huang Chunming, translated by Howard Goldblatt, Copyright ©2001 Columbia University Press. Reprinted with permission of the publisher.

Other stories first published in English by Balestier Press in 2021

Sponsored by Ministry of Culture, Republic of China (Taiwan)

ISBN 978 1 911221 15 9

All rights reserved. No part of this publication may be reproduced, stored in a retrieval system or transmitted in any form or by any means, electronic, mechanical, without the prior written permission of the publisher of this book.

This book is a work of fiction. The literary perceptions and insights are based on experience, all names, characters, places, and incidents either are products of the author's imagination or are used fictitiously.

Contents

The Street Sweeper's Son *7*

Young Bach *13*

Northgate Avenue *17*

Raise the Bottles *23*

Got a Light? *29*

Playing with Fire *38*

Fat Auntie *44*

A Man and His Pocketknife *50*

Follow My Feet *73*

The Face in the Mirror *109*

Damn—It's, Misery! *116*

A Headless Wasp *125*

The Gong *135*

Uncle Gan Geng at Dusk *233*

The Street Sweeper's Son[1]

Mr. Xie of the Third Section, Fourth Grade was worried again, that was obvious. He wondered if some sort of enmity had existed between him and Liu Jizhao in a previous life. The boy could not rest unless he'd given his teacher a headache several times a day.

Jizhao was smart and mischievous—he was a kid who loved to play. Maybe he was small and wore the look of poverty, but in the limited world of the school he was a literary giant, an artist, an athlete, and there was no form of antics he had not mastered. That little head of his was the repository of a subtle philosophy: he believed that people were put on this earth to hop and skip and play games. Mr. Xie had been on the lookout for an opportunity

---

[1] This story was originally published on 12 December 1956, when the author was a student at a college in southern Taiwan. It was his first published story.

to teach the boy a lesson, but that opportunity remained out of reach. Homework? He did it, and better than his fellow students. He was inquisitive, and asked about everything, almost as if he were trying to show up the teacher, who could not refuse to answer students' questions. To make things worse, his questions were based on fact and reason. There were times when he was totally out of control, but never in class.

Then one day bad luck came his way. The teacher caught him spitting and tossing litter on the floor. To that was added using a dialect when speaking,[2] and not only ignoring the advice of the class leader, but hitting the boy and telling him to mind his own business.

Just before class let out, Mr. Xie stood at the podium, his square face set, and said: "Boys and girls, I want to ask you something." He paused. "Is it all right to spit anywhere you like?"

"No!" they responded in unison.

"How about littering?"

"No!"

"Should we hit people?"

"No, we shouldn't."

"Liu Jizhao, stand up," Xie demanded. "This boy was guilty of all those things today," he continued. "But I don't plan to give him demerits. Instead, I'm going to have him sweep the classroom by himself." When the punishment was announced, all eyes shifted to Liu Jizhao. Some students giggled, others pretended to be applauding him, and still others, those who had suffered the most at his hands, assumed an expression that showed their satisfaction

---

[2] During the early days of martial law in Taiwan, students were forced to use only Mandarin in school; the use of the Taiwanese local language was a cause for discipline.

with the punishment. Jizhao kept his head down.

"All right, class dismissed."

"Stand up! Bow! Dismissed!" announced the class leader. Bedlam followed, with applause, shouts, banging on desks, and a general uproar.

Mr. Xie left the classroom, but returned and walked up to Jizhao. "When you've finished sweeping, come to my office. I want to check what you've done. If it's not up to par, you'll have to do it again. You cannot go home until you've passed my inspection. Understand? All right, you may begin."

He turned and walked away. The boy gestured, pretending to use his fists on the teacher's back, and once the teacher was out of earshot, Jizhao cursed him under his breath. Then he turned to look at the classroom, which was dirtier and messier than usual, because classmates who were not his friends had torn up paper and scattered the scraps around. Some had even wiped slobber and snot on the walls and left their shoe prints on desks and chairs. He turned angry-red when he saw what they had done and vented his fury on those desks and chairs, flinging them all over the place. But then it dawned on him that it was getting late, and all the other students had gone home. A temper tantrum would only make things worse, so he picked up the broom and started sweeping. It took lots of time and plenty of sweat, but he managed to finish, more or less, just as Mr. Xie showed up.

"What's this? After all this time this is the best you can do?" Mr. Xie commented as he walked up. "Has it been fun?" He paused. "All right, no more mischief, understand? Any more of that and you'll sweep out the classroom every day. It's late, so hurry home."

Jizhao was in a foul mood all the way home. Being forced to sweep the floor had made him very unhappy, and he vowed not to change his unruly ways. There is a big difference between work and play, he believed. Work is sordid, play is noble. The teacher had made him sweep the floor because he had confused the two.

He arrived home at dinnertime—families without electricity ate dinner early—and his worried mother asked why he was so late. He placated her with a story he'd made up on the walk home. Then, famished, he put away his school bag, sat down, and began eating.

"Jizhao, your father isn't home yet, so leave something for him," she said tenderly.

"Where is he, Ma?" He hadn't thought about his father until his mother mentioned him. He was unbelievably hungry.

"He's not back from work yet."

He quickly finished dinner and helped took his younger brother for a walk in the yard. It was getting dark, and he wondered why his father still wasn't home. Images of the man floated into his young mind: picking up garbage from the city's streets and lanes, sweeping roadways and tidying up ditches, cleaning public toilets, and the like. Given his active imagination, Jizhao was absorbed in wide-ranging thoughts. Each day at the crack of dawn, Papa put on his blue uniform with the white number and conical bamboo hat and did not return home until the sun had settled behind the mountain. Why did he have to go out and sweep up after people every day? Yes, from the moment Jizhao had gained an understanding of people's lives, Papa had earned a living as a street sweeper. What had he done wrong? Who had inflicted that punishment on him? His teacher? *That's funny, I never saw Papa go to school and never heard him mention a teacher. Why doesn't Qixin's papa sweep streets for other people? He once did a very bad thing—he beat Qixin's mother senseless. But he dresses up every morning and rides a pedicab to the bank on Zhongzheng Road, and then returns home in a pedicab at night with lots of money, proud as can be. He gives Qixin money all the time, buys him new shoes, and takes him to the movies. Papa says we're poor, so why aren't they poor? Papa probably goes out to sweep streets because we're poor. But Ah-tian's papa is poor, too, so why isn't he a street sweeper? His papa gets up early to buy fish at the market to peddle around town, and he doesn't return home till late. Ah-tian says his papa sells fish because they're poor. Ah-tian gave me a fish once. It was delicious. He said they eat fish every day. That sounds wonderful. It would be great if Papa could quit being a street sweeper and start selling fish. What did he do that was so bad? Ruilong's papa does better than Papa, too. He often helps Ruilong with his math at home and buys magazines like* Young Learners *and* Eastern Youths *for him. And then there are Xitang's papa, Huixiong's papa ... the papas of every kid in my class all do better than mine, since they don't have to sweep the streets. Papa must have done something terrible!* Jizhao was crying by the time his thoughts reached this point, when he spotted Papa's blurred figure at the bottom of the hill, pulling his handcart behind him. Papa waved to Jizhao to come help him pull the cart up the hill. When they made it home, he praised Jizhao for being a good boy, and strong, as he reached into his pocket and took out three coins. "Here, these are for you. I found them when I was cleaning one of the ditches."

"I don't need money, Papa." Jizhao turned and ran off. Papa was pleased to see what a sensible boy his son was.

Jizhao ran to be alone so he could bawl his eyes out. *What can I do—Papa is a lawbreaker. My teacher made me sweep the floor because I did something bad today. What does that say about Papa? He sweeps the streets, so he must be a lawbreaker. From now on, the other kids at school will laugh at me for having a lawbreaker as a father ...* It was getting dark by then, bedtime, so he carried his brother back inside.

He slept fitfully that night, with his classmates' faces floating in and out of his head, always laughing at him—even in his dreams. Getting through the long night was torture.

The next morning he left for school, terrified and hobbled by a sense of inferiority. His heart skipped a beat when the school gate came into view, and he was reminded of all those laughing faces. He stopped, afraid to go in. Some of his classmates walked by and smiled at him, which made him more anxious than ever. *I knew it. I knew they'd laugh at me. I can't go to class, they'll laugh their heads off. No, no! I can't go to class! Oh, here comes Qixin, and he's smiling at me ...*

Jizhao's fears surged. He turned and ran.

1956

Young Bach

Ever since the previous week, when I had begun substitute teaching for Mr. Chen, the children in this third-year class had pestered me to tell them stories.

I'd held them off as long as I could. They knew how to read music and had an ear for it, so today, after finishing the lesson during our fourth class, I decided to tell them a story after all, since there were still ten minutes left.

"I'll tell you a story about a musician. He was the composer of 'The Old Fisherman,' which we just studied."

The children whooped their delight.

"All right, then, no talking."

They saw this as a fair trade-off and stopped talking. Forty-eight pairs of bright, eager eyes gazed expectantly at me. I turned and wrote "Ba Ha" on the blackboard.

"Today I'm going to tell you about this man, Ba Ha. We'll hear how an industrious little boy grew up to be a famous composer." I heard giggles.

"The composer's name was Ba, like Baba, Ha as in ha-ha. Ba Ha Baba, Baba Ba Ha."

"Making him sound like Papa is cool. So let's call him Papa. That's funny." They all laughed.

"All right, that's enough, quiet down."

"Stop laughing," an impatient student said, "or he won't tell us the story."

The classroom went quiet. All those lovely, curious little faces waiting to hear a story about Ba Ha.

"Yes, this composer was called Ba Ha. He was the papa of music, but most people don't call him that. They call him the *father* of music." I took advantage of their reaction to help relate to their own memories.

"Bach, which was his name in German, enjoyed a wonderful childhood. That was because his papa and mama loved him. So did his brother. He was very smart. Think for a moment what a happy family that was. Just like yours, isn't that right?" Every face wore a contented smile.

"But before long that happiness ended, when the angel of death took his beloved papa and mama, one right after the other." I lowered my voice, stopped, and looked at them. The angel of death appeared to have ripped the smiles off their faces and replaced them with worried looks.

"Children," I rushed to ease their concern, "how lucky you are. You have parents and brothers and sisters who love you." Their happiness returned.

"Teacher," Qingshui said as he stood up and pointed to Xiuming, who was sitting near him, "he doesn't have parents.

He lives with his older brother." Now, this was awkward. Having taken over the class only days before, I knew nothing about their families. Should I have at least made an attempt?

Xiuming was obviously hurt. He ducked his head under his desk and sobbed.

If what Qingshui said was true, the boy's gaunt figure and tattered, ill-fitting clothes were all I needed to see to know how his older brother was treating him. For a moment I stood there stumped for a reaction, and I could tell how flustered I appeared by the look in the children's eyes. Once I went back to telling the story, I had obviously lost my audience. Maybe they were thinking, *How come the teacher is ignoring Xiuming? See how sad he is?* I had no choice but to accept my gaffe and make the best of it. So, back to the story:

"… poor little Bach moved in with his brother. He had lost his mother and father, but his teacher loved him, and he had many friends. They went to class together, played together, had wonderful times together …"

"Living with his brother felt strange at first. Since everything was new, he caused a bit of trouble, and his brother scolded him, even hit him. But it was for his own good, something to help him be a good boy …" I stole a glance at Xiuming, who had stopped crying and was sitting up playing with a pencil. That helped.

The children were caught up in the story I was effectively concocting, so I threw myself into it: "… He stole a musical score from his brother's room and went up to the roof to copy it by the light of the moon so he could secretly learn from his brother. But his brother discovered his secret one day, and not only beat him severely but threw the notebook into which he'd painstakingly copied the musical score into the fire …"

"... But he was blessed with perseverance and courage. Nothing could stop him from studying music. And he learned his lessons well, becoming a great composer. People these days honor him with the title 'The Father of Music.'"

The children showed their pleasure by clapping.

"Bach, Papa," they chanted, "the papa of music, the father of music." It was a lighthearted chorus; even Xiuming was happy. The bell sounded, so they picked up their school bags and walked out of the room singing "The Old Fisherman."

I sat down, wiped the sweat from my forehead, and drank some water.

"Teacher." It was a tiny voice. I turned to the door, and there stood Xiuming. I gulped in surprise, but waved him in. "Come in, Xiuming."

He didn't move. When I repeated myself, he cocked his head, tugged at his jacket, and inched his way toward me.

"What is it, Xiuming?" Now he was standing in front of me, staring at his feet and fidgeting. I reached over and wiped his runny nose with a tissue.

"Teacher—" His voice was still soft, with a slight stammer. "I— could I be like Bach someday?" With a furrowed brow, he looked at me with his head cocked to one side. I was so touched I couldn't speak. I crouched down, took his little hand in mine, and nodded. Nearly in tears, I fought to keep from crying so he wouldn't doubt that I meant it. But my sense of compassion was so strong that two teardrops fell from my eyes. It was an occasion replete with happiness, a time for smiling. At that moment, in my eyes he was only a thin, blurry, shadow-like figure.

1957

Northgate Avenue

There he was again. Every day, right around sunset. As always, he was sitting on a fire department box at a Northgate Avenue intersection, like a statue, hardly moving, his vacant, bloodshot eyes fixed on the pharmacy across the street. He wore a somber, troubled look. His feeble, dejected appearance, his protruding cheekbones, and his tattered rain hat were obvious signs of his impoverished state. A lit New Paradise cigarette either dangled from his lips or was caught between two fingers. We never saw one without the other.

On rainy days he moved under an awning and leaned against a column, arms folded across his chest, eyes still fixed on the same old spot. This had been going on for months.

For years he had worked hard and saved up enough after the war to buy a rundown property on Northgate Avenue. He'd fixed it up to accommodate a family of seven. That had relieved him of a heavy burden, for he had suffered guilt feelings over subjecting his wife and children to such a rootless life.

Northgate Avenue was the heart of the town. He often congratulated himself and shuddered to think about his indecision prior to the purchase. What if he hadn't bought it? He didn't want to think about that. The truth was, he had bought it, with the fruits of his bitter labor, and that was an indisputable fact.

He had laid out a plan: renting out the front of the house for someone to open a shop would bring in at least a thousand a month; his oldest son, who worked in a government office, brought in four or five hundred after paying for food; son number two would find a job after his military service. So for now sons three through five were the main concern. *Though my income as a Taoist priest is not fixed, I can count on six or seven hundred a month, so we have a pretty good life.*

His plans had reached fruition within a short time, and he was somewhat better off than before. He could enjoy a drink and a snack to go with it every evening. Then, after dinner, he picked his teeth, drank a cup of green tea, smoked a cigarette, took a walk, and went to see friends or took in a movie. If a man could live like an artist, then he was one, for during his free moments he took breaks from his daily routine to quietly admire a creation he had been working on for decades; it was coming along nicely. He paid no attention to the criticisms of others. The pleasure in creating art lies not just in its completion, but also in the many subtle emotional reactions it engenders.

Time dilutes longstanding pleasures, which are replaced by new impulses. The desire to seek satisfaction in new pleasures is especially strong among the young.

"Ah-pa ..." Eldest Son stammered, then swallowed what he was going to say.

"Hm—" A low, nasal response symbolized a father's authority.

"Can we go inside?" the young man said softly. "I need to talk to you about something."

Eldest Son went in first and chased his younger brothers out. He and his father sat down to talk.

The old man wondered what this was all about, since his son was not the secretive type. Had something bad happened? It was clearly bothering the son, and that gave the father a bad feeling. His nerves were suddenly on edge.

"I'm in trouble again," he said weakly, the sound of a despondent young man. His palms were sweaty as he looked his father in the eye.

The old man let his gaze settle elsewhere, with no response to what he'd just heard. His chest heaved, and his anxiety rose.

"My idea was to recoup everything from the previous times, and going bust again was the last thing on my mind," Eldest Son said through clenched teeth. "This time it was Japanese pharmaceuticals, tens of thousands, all gone."

The old man didn't make a sound. Truth is, the words "tens of thousands" had all but paralyzed him. Where was he going to get that much? The realization that the house was worth tens of thousands was like a punch in the gut.

"I think ..." Eldest Son assumed that the old man had not been paying attention. "Ah-pa!" he said, louder this time. "Are you listening?" Suddenly regretting that, he softened his tone: "I'm sorry. I shouldn't talk to you that way. But ... I wanted to help improve the family's finances, so you could retire. That's why ..." He couldn't go on. He broke down and wept.

The silence over the next few moments was broken only by the sobs of Eldest Son, who was bent over the table. The old man sympathized with his son, who was the beneficiary of a father's unspoken love, though he did not know that. The old man felt no need to express it in terms other than "Are you cold?" "Are you hungry?" The sort of love a mother bestows upon her children.

His lips parted and quivered a moment before he was able to speak. "I've always known that you and your brothers feel that Taoist priest is not a noble profession, that it is behind the times. You feel you can't hold your heads up with a father like me, when in fact this profession has made it possible for you to be where you are today." Still looking at the same spot, he continued slowly: "You think I have a lowly job, but many people feel that I bring them comfort, something on which they can pin their hopes. I lack your vision and don't see myself as rough around the edges. I tell you that the eighteen levels of Hell are the punishment that awaits unfilial sons like you." He fought to control the bitterness filling his chest. His lips quivered so hard he couldn't close them.

He understood the mentality of the young, but at this moment he found it hard to accept. He was a fount of knowledge, gained from his daily routine of reading the newspaper. Troubled by what he'd just said, he sensed that he had betrayed his own conscience. In recent years he'd developed misgivings about his beliefs.

"I made it clear to you when you decided to take this on. 'Qingchi,' I said, 'this is no business to get involved in. The days when you could make a killing this way have passed. Doing it now is a losing proposition.' Think back, did I or did I not say that? But you wouldn't listen. Now see what's happened. I can't …"

"I didn't come back to get a lecture," Qingchi interrupted him, jerking his head up and pounding the table before angrily walking out.

The old man's head was swimming; everything in front of him had been swallowed up in darkness.

This unexpected blow had not floored him, but it came close.

His wife was a worrier—how was he going to keep something this big from her? His hands were tied; he would have to sell the house. Knowing that was one thing; accepting it was another. Buying it had been his good fortune; selling it would be his fate. But he had been able to make do without the house once, hadn't he? He tried hard to console himself, to change his mindset and accept the new reality, but that was nearly impossible. He fell into a deep, ineffable depression.

***

Before long, the sale of the house, Qingchi's suicide, his wife's melancholia, his third son dropping out of school to help, and being forced to move into a relative's farmhouse were all his fault, he felt. He thought about ending it all, but his conscience and his sense of responsibility would not let him do that. At the very least, he would have to wait until son number two came home and found work. Day after troubling day led to a state of demoralization, until he could barely think. Thoughts vanished from his head; the conflict between his sense of responsibility and the notion of suicide ceased to exist. His mind a blank, he became a walking corpse.

No one knew why he insisted on sitting in that spot or what went through his mind while he was there. Had it been the same thought for more than a year? Even he wasn't sure, but unlike other people, he never tried to figure that out. It was a sort of obsession and subconscious sense of ownership that led this shell of a man to linger at this one spot.

After a trying year, the family had gotten used to a new normal.

At midnight one day, half the sky turned red.

"Hey, there's a fire in town!" came the shouts.

People woke up and ran to the threshing ground. Like so many other people, he took off toward town.

"Ah-tu," his concerned wife called after him, "where are you going at this hour?" He neither stopped nor turned his head.

"There's a fire on Northgate Avenue." Hearing people talk about the fire, he stepped up the pace, like a machine moving endlessly forward.

There was no mistake—Northgate Avenue was on fire. The funeral supply shop, where the fire had started, had turned to ashes; the fire had spread to the tailor shop, and sparks had ignited the pharmacy and hardware store, as well as the shoe store.

It was like a predatory beast, its flaming tongue engulfing the tailor shop and swallowing it whole. A sea of fire had swamped the pharmacy.

He ran up to the police barricade, but was kept outside the tape. He could only watch as the house on which he had spent his blood and sweat was devoured by the raging inferno. The flames were reflected in crystalline tears at the corners of his eyes as the power of an obsessive love spread through his body. He had, for a short time, enjoyed a life like a beautiful dream in that house, and though it had been taken over by someone else, it had remained a memorable place. He was like a climber at the foot of a mountain gazing with exhilaration up at the peak he has just conquered. He loves its austerity and the danger it poses, for it has the capacity to signify greatness.

When the police were looking elsewhere, he made a mad dash for the pharmacy. A dark figure fell amid the ferocious red flames as the blaze spread, bringing down the pharmacy roof. People in the bustling crowd gazed skyward as the scalding maelstrom carried hot ashes high into the sky.

March 1962

Raise the Bottles

A pair of liquor bottles swung back and forth atop the flagpole at K Middle School, banging against the metal pole and sending forth loud, pleasant clangs that eddied in the early morning air. When the students saw them, they bowed in silent respect to the anonymous hero or heroes responsible for this masterpiece. Despite the stern look, the director of discipline and guidance was secretly amused. *High school kids these days are full of creative mischief and are getting worse.* He had to focus on what he would say at the morning assembly, where he would admonish the perpetrators of this prank. The military instructor held a different view. He considered it more than a mere prank and demanded that the culprits be caught and punished.

***

After "The Blues" ended, she returned unhappily to her seat, wishing she hadn't danced. What she really regretted was dancing with someone else. By that, she meant her good friend. The one she really wanted was in the chair beside her, someone she had met only recently. Though she could already tell he liked her, there was still room for doubt, since she had been disappointed more than once. His forced smile obviously concealed flames of jealousy burning inside. To test him, she faked nonchalance, something she was good at.

"That was a good number. Why weren't you dancing?"

"What's so great about dancing? I'd rather just sit here." What he meant was sit with her, an intention he desperately wanted to convey. She must have missed his meaning, for she did not respond. Tormented by resentment, he said, in a tone dripping with reproach, "I hate seeing you and other guys locked in an embrace."

His suffering gave her the sweet feeling of being loved. But she had to keep warning herself not to reveal her feelings to him.

"How can you say locked in an embrace?" she said. "It's just dancing."

"That's not what those perverts are thinking."

"I'll ask you, are you a pervert?"

"Sometimes. That's how I know what they're thinking."

"You know, you're really selfish. You dance with pretty women, so why does it bother you when I dance with other guys?" She tried to sound angry, but that wasn't how she felt. By the time someone tried to make her his, she already felt that she'd made him hers. If she even gave a hint that she liked someone, that person was transformed into a brooch she could effortlessly pin onto her blouse, while he thought he had made her his. That was love, two people deceiving one another, slightly wild and somewhat primitive.

There was nothing he could say to that. What he wanted to say was, "I love you," but he lacked the nerve. All his addled brain could come up with was, "You're right, but they don't think so. Hell, I don't know." *What a dopey thing to say,* he rebuked himself.

"You're an honest liar," she said with a smile. He got a kick out of her snide little comment, and in the days to follow, he would sign his letters to her "An honest liar."

"You don't like me, do you? I'm not about to pretend I don't have any faults."

"A man without faults is boring, but trying to cover them up unnerves me. And affected guys turn me off. But men like you, who stupidly give up the right to lie to girls …" She ended with almost wanton laughter.

"Well?" he said. She was still laughing. "So?"

"Fascinating. That's what I like about you."

"Really!" Sad no longer, he was barely able to keep from shouting.

"Calm down. Don't get carried away or you'll be disappointed," she said with a cruel edge.

"What do you mean?"

"Hasn't it dawned on you that I've been around and am not some shy little girl? Not completely …"

"Go ahead, say it. That's the kind of woman I like."

"The more the better, is that it?"

"Oh, no! You're the only one."

"I keep a diary sometimes, and I once wrote that I'm like a road sign to decadence. I've sent two people in that direction already, and I don't want you to end up the same way."

"That's what I figured. Last week when you danced with me, I thought I was the one you hoped to fall in love with. It hasn't been all that long, has it?"

"Didn't you get my letter?" he asked anxiously.

"It flew to me like a snowflake. I thought about writing back, but I'm not a truthful letter writer. I exaggerate, and pretend I'm miserable. That's why I didn't write."

Fortunately, the lights in the room and the beat of the music masked the look of embarrassment on his face and the sound of his thumping heart. *Is that how she felt about my letter?* He knew he must say something in response to keep her from noting his embarrassment. But what?

"That really bugs me," he said.

"You need to know that I have lots of boyfriends."

"If you were married with kids, now, *that* would be romantic."

They laughed. A slow tune, "Too Young," came on. Couples got up from their seats and walked hand-in-hand onto the dance floor. He flashed a signal with his eyes. "Shall we?"

They were like a pair of swans gliding gracefully across a lily pond, raising sublime ripples on the surface. Very slowly, his arm encircled her waist; she laid her head against his chest and began humming softly along with the alluring voice of the man singing.

"This is one of the most beautiful songs ever," he said.

His enjoyment of the song was enhanced by the smell of her hair, and even more by her love adhering to his body. He was sinking into an abyss of happiness.

In bed that night, he was so fired up he couldn't sleep. He recalled every minute he'd spent with her and every word they'd spoken. Things had changed since their talk the previous Saturday. If it kept going this way, he'd soon be saying goodbye to his men's dormitory. He thought back on the week before, dwelling on what had happened.

They had met at a party at Wenxiong's house. He thought he'd seen the woman next to him somewhere, so he asked. And he was right—she was Ms. Yang, the practice teacher for his English class the year before. He had given her a grade of ninety-six. She remembered him, too. Wenxiong told him that she had looked at a class picture at his house one day and asked Wenxiong about him. He was mad at Wenxiong for not telling him.

They danced that night, and talked, both trying anything to keep the conversation going. Consciously or not, they revealed what they liked.

"I've heard this cha-cha before," she said, "and it didn't sound like this."

"It's an adaptation of Beethoven's 'Für Elise.' What do you think? Not bad, huh?"

"I'd be surprised if Beethoven isn't turning over in his grave."

"Really? I think he'd give it a thumbs-up. He was the central figure of the Romantic School," he said. "I guess you listen to lots of classical music."

"No, just once in a while. But you must be an authority on the subject."

"Far from it. I just like it," he said. "But I like pop music, too."

"So you're ambivalent."

"Ambivalent or not, I don't care. Music is music. Let's say Papa wears neatly pressed suits, but Big Brother goes casual. Papa scolds Big Brother for being sloppy, Big Brother says Papa is too stuffy. Total nonsense. Besides, popular music is the soul of youth and, like other music, requires talent to create. Without it, the world would lose its vitality." He felt he needed to say more, so before she opened her mouth, he continued: "That's a simple illustration. We need places of entertainment like theaters, bars, coffee shops, dance halls, or so-called clubs. If one day they all switched to classical music, the deadening pall would be unimaginable." He talked the night away and was pleased with how things went, seeing a look of admiration in her eyes.

***

"You really don't want to go?" she asked over the phone.
"Let's go for a late-night snack instead. What do you say?"
"I already accepted their invitation. And I never miss one of their parties."
"That's what bothers me. The place bugs me."
"Up to you. But I'm going."

She hung up. Disappointed, he replaced the handset and went back into his room. A stack of English exercise books from two classes rested on the right side of his desk, and five graded ones were on the left, while between them, a pen with red ink lay on an open exercise book as dejected as he. The wastepaper basket on the floor was filled with torn envelopes, all with the same letterhead. He was surrounded by chaos that matched his mood.

He sat down to continue grading in order to put her out of his mind. It didn't work. Dejectedly, he pushed away the booklet and his pen, knocking over the bottle of red ink, and just let it flow. He turned out the light and lit a cigarette. That didn't help, either, so he went out.

She wasn't at the party. He saw people he knew leaving, and felt better. But only briefly, as his thoughts turned so troubling he felt like crying. He spent the night wandering in a different world, and returned home with two bottles of liquor, stopping along the way at a little diner to buy some beef jerky on credit. He woke up an old classmate, a geography teacher, to eat and drink with him. The moon was out, so he suggested they go to the gym field.

As the night grew late, someone kept repeating a liquor-induced mumble by the flagpole: "Raise the bottles! Raise the bottles!"

The sound of laughter could be heard from the two men.

1963

Got a Light?

He rummaged through three of his four pockets and determined that he'd been too tense, too hurried, to remember his lighter, probably because he thought he had already gone through them.

Dying for a smoke, that was a first for him. Maybe he felt it might help straighten out his tangled thoughts or bring some peace to his unsettled mind. In any case, what he needed now was more than a routine way to kill time. Nothing, he felt, was more essential at this moment than a cigarette. He never objected when people called cigarettes a waste of money, but at this point it was the smartest option. Normally, this sort of analysis would not have occurred to him, but an irrepressible desire had overshadowed all other thoughts and become the one thing he must do before anything else.

Sitting beside him was a similarly middle-aged gentleman well on his way to being portly. He was smoking and reading a newspaper.

"Got a light? May I?" He took the gentleman's cigarette to light his own. "Thanks." After handing it back, he leaned against the window and, turning to look out, was absorbed in his thoughts.

The gentleman retrieved his cigarette without taking his eyes off the local section of the newspaper. Putting it back between his lips, he took a puff; a frown wrinkled his face as he removed the cigarette for a close examination. *This can't be!* There on the butt, encircled by a golden yellow ring, were the words "New Paradise" in florid script. There had been a switch, since he smoked cigarettes with the words "Double Happiness" inside a red ring. He turned to look at his fellow traveler, who was staring out the window, lost in thought. Amused by the sight, he considered his options. Should he pretend there was nothing wrong? After all, it wasn't a decision worthy of much consideration. So, motivated by curiosity and a need to keep from getting bored during the two-hour journey, he carefully put out the cigarette he was holding.

Still looking out the window, the other man took a puff every once in a while, looking as if someone else's hand were putting the smoke in his mouth.

"May I borrow your cigarette?" the gentleman said softly.

The other man remained as motionless as a wooden statue.

The gentleman awkwardly touched his fellow traveler's leg, waving his cigarette when the man turned to look.

"A light, please."

Staring blankly at the seat back in front of him, the other man shifted in his seat to hand his cigarette to the gentleman.

The gentleman lit the cigarette and then took back his own.

GOT A LIGHT?

The other man took a puff off his cigarette and then another, exhaling smoke, first through his nose and then his mouth, which seemed to cheer him for the time being. But he turned back to gaze out the window, as if he were discarding the shell of his body in order to enter a world of his own. Anyone watching would have found this to be an enigmatic sight, no doubt, which was how the gentleman felt. He experienced a bit of a letdown, for he had been secretly watching the other man, certain he would be surprised to discover he'd gotten his own cigarette back. But it did not register.

The express train sped across the Lanyang Plain, expected to arrive at his destination on time; but his thoughts were roaming through a different time and space, something that was not expected.

Earlier that morning, he had received an express letter from Kangming at school, and he was more worried than his son tried to sound in the letter. Fully aware of the boy's temperament, he knew that even facing the guillotine would not trouble him all that much. He'd read the letter without fully grasping its meaning. This is what Kangming had written:

Papa,

I'm really sorry I've let you down. In all honesty, I've always wanted to be a good son, especially since that time I saw how hurt you were when I received two demerits for fighting. I've told myself since then all I want is to be a good boy and make you happy. But I've done it again.

We had yesterday afternoon off. The military instructor had asked for a leave of absence, so both his classes were canceled, and we were supposed to busy ourselves with extracurricular activities. Well, I went with some classmates to see a Japanese film called The

Meiji Emperor and the Russo-Japanese War. *Someone ratted on us, and now the school authorities are going to hold a disciplinary meeting to decide what to do with me, since I already had two demerits on my record. The director of discipline called me in to say that I'll be expelled. He said my national consciousness was weak, and I believe that's the main reason for my expulsion. Papa, what is national consciousness? To be honest, I don't know what it means.*

My homeroom teacher said you should probably come, but I don't think you need to. Let them expel me, I don't care. I'd rather be a good son at home than an obedient student at school. Please don't make the trip, Papa.

Your son,

Kangming.

Taken separately, the words "national consciousness" are easy to understand, but when put together they are hard to fathom. He thought long and hard, but still could not figure it out. It must have something to do with the film and the Meiji emperor, he told himself, and that might make it a major offense, since they'd mentioned "national." That was all he could come up with. Having only finished primary school, he had done his best to give his children the finest education possible.

After reading the letter, he had checked the time and seen that he could make the ten o'clock northbound express. So he'd put aside his work at his shop and rushed to Taipei.

Strange though it may sound, of all his children, he favored the second son, who did not like school, had received enough demerits to be expelled, and caused him plenty of trouble and many headaches. Apparently the boy was a carbon copy of him, while the other two took after their weepy mother in appearance as well as their tendency to tear up over the smallest thing; they could choke up even when talking. He hated boys who acted like that.

He was still more than an hour away from his destination, an impossibly long time in his mind, as if he had to traverse a vast, boundless space on an arduous trek that he must make for his son's sake. Exhausted mentally and physically, he felt discouraged. He worried too much about the boy, he told himself; he wouldn't have to suffer like this if he could just ignore Kangming and let them expel him. Why force him to study if he doesn't want to? The boy could come home to learn a trade and might have a bright future. Some people actually see their future prospects ruined when they are forced to attend a school that's wrong for them. *Kangming could be one of those, I know, for that's how he is,* he told himself, finally feeling a sense of calm take hold of his troubled mind.

A bitter taste told him he was smoking too much. So he tossed the half-smoked cigarette out the window. Now he no longer looked like a wooden statue, as he was able to see the green rice sprouts growing lushly in the field. A sudden loneliness came over him, and he wished he had a friend to talk to. The first thing he'd tell that friend was that spring was finally here, after a winter that might have been the coldest in half a century. Everything outside the window interested him, but the scenery flew past before he could call out the place names. He looked off into the horizon, aimlessly searching for something more interesting.

After pulling his head back in, he took out another cigarette and glanced at his neighbor, who had stopped smoking. He patted his pockets unconsciously before reaching into the last pocket on the right to retrieve his lighter. With the cigarette lit, he turned into a statue again, frozen in an agitated, worried state as a jumble of thoughts entered his head.

Kangming is nineteen, and the best thing for him is still to go to school, no matter what. What exactly does it mean to have a weak national consciousness? Will he be expelled over that? I'll ask his teacher for help. I'll give him something, money maybe. I'll borrow a thousand NT from the owner of the Ruirong Shop as soon as I get to Taipei.

The train compartment was bright, warmed by the early spring weather. Yet his troubled mind and indecision made him hot one moment and cold the next, even dizzy at times. It was a constant struggle to maintain his equilibrium along the way to Taipei and to Kangming's school.

He did not have to wait long in the reception room before fourth period was over and Kangming, who had been notified of his arrival, showed up. Sitting across from his father, the boy looked out of sorts; he had expected a tongue-lashing, but that did not happen. The first thing his father said when he saw Kangming was, "You're quite the kid, aren't you?" He continued with a weary smile as he sized the boy up. "You haven't changed. I don't think you ever will. Didn't I tell you not to alter your uniform? Look at your pants. Aren't those bell-bottoms? Is your memory really that short? Have you forgotten that I've cut up clothes like that in the past?"

The boy looked down, rubbing his hands back and forth on his knees.

"What's going on now?"

Kangming looked up and said, "My homeroom teacher said the principal went to a meeting down south, and he won't know anything until the principal returns." He added after a momentary hesitation, "I want to quit school, Papa."

"I knew you'd say that. You need to stay in school, for me if not for yourself." He wanted to tell the boy why that was, but there were other people around, and he didn't have much time. "We'll talk about that later. Let's go see your homeroom teacher first."

They went to the teacher's house, and after some small talk, he said, "Kangming has caused you headaches. I'm so sorry. I had little schooling and can barely read, and we live far away, so I'm asking you to help keep the boy in check. You can hit him if he misbehaves, and I won't say a word. We really need your help with what happened yesterday. Please help us." He told his son to interpret what he said, but the teacher switched to Taiwanese when Kangming hesitated. "That's not necessary. I speak Taiwanese."

After his repeated plea, the teacher arrived at a solution. "Go see the discipline director before he leaves for a meeting. I'll tell you what to say and will talk to him when he returns."

Before they left, the father handed the teacher an envelope with money; the teacher would not take it, but said nothing when it was left on the table.

"Don't tell him you've been to see me." The teacher stopped them before they walked out. "I'll talk to him when he's back from his meeting."

They rushed to the director's house. Kangming was disgruntled that his father was being so obsequious, but there was nothing he could do about it.

At the director's house his father repeated what he'd said earlier, adding what the teacher had told him to say.

The director seemed to give the matter serious consideration. So the father took out an envelope, saying it was a token of his gratitude, despite a firm refusal from the director, who did not object when the father gave the money to a child playing next to them.

"Good. Go see your teacher," the director said. "But don't tell him you've been to see me. I'll talk to him when I get back from a meeting this afternoon."

Years of work experience told the father that everything was fine and that his son would not be expelled. "I think you'll be fine now," he said with a smile when they left the house, "but I want you to behave yourself until the day you finish high school. Let's go see your teacher, so I can head back today."

He managed to catch the 7:50 local train for Su-ao. No one he knew was on the train, so he smoked and pondered his business and money situation, both of which took up so much of his time each day that he couldn't stop thinking about them. They were boring matters, but he could not find anything else to occupy his mind. The passenger beside him, a man in black-framed glasses, had his head buried in a book. A hint of envy rose up inside. The man must be well read, so he said, "Excuse me, sir. Can you tell me what it means to have a weak national consciousness?" He was surprised by the impulse to ask.

Staring blankly at him, the man in the glasses asked why he'd asked that. He said it was nothing, he was just curious. After a momentary pause, the man decided that the father was testing him, so he said unhappily, "A weak national consciousness refers to people who don't know what it means to have a weak national consciousness." He returned to his book, feeling secretly smug.

The father thanked him, feeling both enlightened and more confused than ever. It did not matter any longer, now that Kangming was fine, however, so he put it out of his mind.

It was a long trip, and with the train stopping at every small station, the ride was the embodiment of boredom. A couple sitting up ahead was talking, so he cocked his head slightly to eavesdrop.

"I've told you already," the woman said. "I won't."

"What's the big deal? Why must you act like this?"

"What day is tomorrow?"

"Come on, why won't you say yes?" The man persisted.

He had no idea what they were talking about. From where he sat, he could see the top halves of their heads resting against the seat back, constantly coming together and moving away. They looked intimate, a sight that sent a stirring through his heart. He laughed and said to himself, *Why not use this opportunity to put one over on my wife?* He could go home the next day. He made up his mind to get off at Jiaoxi, where he would enjoy a bath at the hot springs before showing himself a good time.

He got off at Jiaoxi. Standing on the platform, as the train pulled out of the station, he mumbled to himself, "Wow, I actually got off! I'll be damned."

The neon lights at Bishan Villa blinked seductively, reminding him of something he'd heard about the place, that the girls all had lovely figures.

1963

Playing with Fire

It was only late spring, but already blazing summer-hot. All the fans in the local express car were on high, and still passengers were trying frantically to cool themselves with hand-held fans. Most of them, not counting the children, sprawled lethargically against the backs of their seats in the stifling heat.

Tightly shut blinds blocked the sun's blistering rays from the west and a view of trees zipping past the window, drawing loud complaints from a child who wanted to see outside. Hoping to mollify him, his father substituted his cigarette lighter for the passing scenery.

"Don't let him play with that," the mother scolded.

"He'll cry if you take it away from him. See how much fun he's having?"

The boy could not get it to light no matter how many times he flicked the wheel, but he soldiered on, trying first with one hand and then with the other.

"I don't know why playing with fire is so much fun, but I was taught to be careful with it."

"He'll learn when he burns his finger. After that he'll be careful."

"No more of your naturalist philosophy, please. You're spoiling him."

"May I suggest that a wife should not know more than her husband?"

The young couple laughed together.

Their son sat next to them like a scientist engrossed in an experiment, hoping to solve the mystery of getting flames to emerge from the lighter he was flicking over and over.

As the train pulled out of the station, new passengers found seats. The suffocating heat sapped their vitality as they leaned back, looking like tuna in a fishmonger's stall.

Hurried footsteps that seemed out of place sounded from the first car to the last and back, stopping with the selection of a satisfactory seat, a trip that breathed life into the languid passengers, most notably the man in the seat directly opposite, who was now on full alert.

A fair-skinned, neatly dressed woman with a fine figure was the perfect remedy for the lassitude that had befallen her fellow passengers. Her white high heels and a necklace of black beads created a stunning contrast; a pair of mirror-lens sunglasses further heightened her allure.

She was secretly delighted over thoughts of what she would soon be enjoying. Every Saturday afternoon after work she took the train to Luodong, making a point of sitting with the men, inflaming them with her obvious charm and looking forward to the embarrassment and awkward conduct that would be brought out by things like desire, unease, uncertainty, anxiety, and rudeness. That gave her a gleeful sense of conquest. When she was home, this was what she and her friends talked about.

The Saturday before, a fidgety, squirming young fellow from Yilan had shrunk back each time he was about to say something, until finally he found the courage to speak, but in a squeaky, quavering voice. She ignored him, he blushed, and then, embarrassed, turned to see if anyone was watching. She pretended to bump him with her foot, but he did not flinch. She pressed on, and after a few moments, like a balloon filled to capacity, he began to wobble, in danger of floating away if the string broke. As a result, he missed his stop and followed her all the way to Luodong. At the ticket gate he had an animated conversation with the clerk, trying to explain what had happened. She turned and looked back from a distance, secretly delighted.

Then there were those impudent, aggressive men who thought so highly of themselves. Them too she found laughable and pitiful. "Men who lose their sense of judgment deserve only to eat bananas," she said caustically to a friend.

"Why?"

"Because they're apes."

On this day she saw through a man who kept swallowing his saliva. This guy, she was thinking, is destined to be another ant on a hot skillet. This will be fun. She leisurely moved to sit down.

"Careful," he said, "the seat's dirty." He handed her a sheet of newspaper. "Here, wipe it with this."

"Thank you," she said with a measure of surprise. Anyone that attentive, she was thinking, had to be a skirt-chaser. She was fully on her guard.

"Where are you headed, miss? Yilan? Luodong? Su-ao?" He waited for an answer before continuing: "You look like a city girl."

She didn't respond. Turning to look out the window, she kept her eye on him from behind her sunglasses and fanned her chest with a handkerchief.

"Sure is hot!" he said as he too fanned himself, sending some of the air her way. "Scientists say it's gotten hotter in recent years, all because the Americans and Russians keep testing nuclear weapons."

She turned all the way toward the window and ignored him.

But a moment later, when she turned back to face front, he doggedly attempted to strike up a conversation with this handsome woman.

"What do you do?" He paused. "Ah, don't tell me. You're a fashion model."

That was funny. She couldn't help smiling.

"That was a good guess, wasn't it?" Truth was, the modeling profession had not yet taken hold in Taiwan. He was trying to get a rise out of her so she would say something.

"Well? Not bad, huh?"

"Meaning?" She could not hold out any longer. Deep down she was pleased. Why? Because she knew that her face was the reason for his speculation.

"Because one look at how you're dressed and your lovely face tell me that has to be your profession."

"You're mocking me. I don't know what to say."

"It's you who's mocking me."

They both laughed.

Mission accomplished. He'd broken the ice and felt that a romance was definitely possible. This was not at all what she'd had in mind. And so they started talking, him taking the lead, her passively following.

He had planned to go to the mineral springs at Jiaoxi, but was still aboard when the train left the station.

"After all this time, we still don't know each other's name. Let me introduce myself. I'm Chen Songnian, I live in Taipei, I'm a graduate from an English-language junior college and recently completed my obligatory military service. I'm still looking for the right job." The detailed introduction was intended to get her to do the same. "I don't yet know your lovely name, but I'm willing to bet it's perfect for you."

Her wariness of men was forgotten thanks to his way with words and his good looks. "My name's Xu Yue'er. I'm on my way home to Luodong from the office."

"No wonder you're so beautiful, with a name like 'Moon.'"

The smile never left her face as she listened to him.

"Have you seen the movie *Strangers When We Meet*, with Kirk Douglas and Kim Novak?"

She nodded.

"It's one of my favorites," he said as he launched into a critique of love and morality, wanting to show her how clever he was. "That's us, isn't it? Strangers when we meet. I was supposed to get off the train at Jiaoxi, but I decided not to, not wanting us to go our separate ways. I'd like to visit Luodong myself. Would you show me around?"

She tensed up, wanting to say no, but ... she didn't know what to do or say.

All of a sudden, a little boy near them burst into tears from burning his hand with the cigarette lighter. "I told you not to play with that," his mother said. "Well, you can burn yourself up for all I care!" She didn't mean that; she was just worried he might have really burned his hand. But he was fine.

"Here, try some more!" She flicked the lighter and held it up close to frighten him. He threw himself into his father's arms and buried his head.

"Ha. My *Émile*," the man quipped in dramatic fashion. She laughed.

The train moved along as silence spread through the car. People caught up in that silence seemed in need of further stimulation.

Woo-woo! Luodong was up ahead.

1963

Fat Auntie

You'd cry as if you'd lost someone near and dear if you thought more about people like us, even small creatures that seem intelligent in your view, if your gaze fell upon a stiff, cold body on the ground. The degree and nature of the emotion would embrace the same sadness, for life is worth cherishing and we mourn a death no matter what.

Not to mention the fact that she was my aunt. I was a week late returning home, and she was resting peacefully in a newly filled grave. A pair of white dahlia wreaths had wilted on the site, their leaves now brown and pulpy from a shower the night before.

Yashu and I were sitting on a nearby grave, smiling through our tears, holding a silent conversation. We knew what each other was thinking, was saying, was answering, but I could not tell if we were sad or not. We just let our emotions flow naturally. I was reminiscing about the past, which seemed like yesterday. They were happy days, weren't they?

"Do you think Auntie really laughed herself to death, Ah-shu?"

"My uncle said she did." A large teardrop rolled down her cheek. "It was lunchtime, and, like every other day, they were talking and eating. He told her a joke that got her laughing. A bit later, when she stood up to get some water, she fell backward with a thud. She was dead by the time the doctor arrived."

"It was a stroke."

"That's what the doctor said, but strokes don't often cause a quick death like that. The real cause was when she hit her head on the floor."

"What was the joke your uncle told her that caused the fatal reaction?"

"You know how my mom loved to laugh. My uncle said he was afraid of ghosts. Once when he was traveling alone at night, he was singing and shouting to boost his courage, but he ended up scaring a kid in a roadside house into crying. The kid's parents came out and screamed at him, 'The ghost will come after you!' My uncle was so frightened he ran home, losing his wooden clogs along the way."

The Grim Reaper has a good sense of humor if that was the joke that caused Auntie's death, I said to myself.

"So she didn't say anything? I mean las words for you before she died?" I asked.

"No. My uncle said she stopped breathing before she could say anything."

"I see. So she probably didn't know she was dying." I paused. "What do you think she'd have said if she'd had the time?"

Yashu was quiet, seemingly lost in thought, her head down.

"I know what she'd say."

She looked up at me, eagerly waiting for me to tell her.

"She might spew out a long string of unpleasant, boring words, like always. But you could sum up everything she said in one phrase—'I love you.'"

Dispirited, Yashu lowered her head; her expression seemed to say, *I don't need you to tell me that.* I knew, too. I also knew she hated me.

Her sadness affected my mood, and soon I was as wretched as she was. The bleak air around us was shrouded in dark-green smoke from three sticks of sandalwood incense (Auntie's favorite for offering to deities and Buddhas) that enmeshed our unspoken thoughts. I could almost hear her say to me, "Go buy a bundle of incense, Ah-sun. Make sure it's the dark sandalwood type, and don't worry about the cost. Nothing else will do." She came to the door as I walked off and shouted, "If they're out, don't buy a substitute, Ah-sun."

Why did she have to keep calling me Ah-sun, little grandson, now that I was a grown man? Maybe she wanted to attract people's attention. *See there! That schoolteacher is my Ah-sun.* She was proud of me, but I lowered my burning red face and quickened my pace.

Even as a kid, I'd heard my parents talk about an aunt in Kaohsiung, someone I had yet to meet. She'd moved back to Luodong with Yashu and an adult brother-in-law the year before, when her husband left home to work in the Philippines.

Auntie was astonishingly fat, so obese her eyes and neck were nearly hidden, their existence reduced to slits. I was shocked when I saw her sitting in the living room. *Where did this circus fat lady come from?* I asked myself. I realized who she was when my father told me to call her Auntie. But I didn't want to; it was too much for me. Why did she have to be my aunt? My friends would make fun of me.

Auntie was pleased to see all five grown children. "If only their mother hadn't died so young, she'd be overjoyed to see them like this," she said. Her face was too fleshy to be expressive. She went quiet for a moment before asking, "How old are you, Ah-sun?" She pointed to me.

I looked at her while Father answered for all of us. "The oldest one is twenty-three, the second one, a girl, twenty-two, the third one, a boy, twenty-one, then twenty and nineteen." Father took great pleasure in showing us off to outsiders. Auntie laughed and said, "My kid brother is so lucky. They should be getting married soon, shouldn't they?"

I heard some snickering.

"You can be their matchmaker," Father joked.

"No problem. I'll do it. I'll find a fair, I mean—a pretty girl with fair skin—for my Ah-sun."

We were all grateful for her reply—melodramatic, sounding more like an actor's line, which meant we could laugh and avoid being called rude by our father. Auntie looked limp from laughing happily. "These five Ah-suns are terrific," she said with a hint of envy.

That was followed by a farcical performance. She wanted to get up, but her enormous backside was stuck between the armrests of the rattan chair, so she struggled, flailing her stumpy arms, but nothing happened. It took a lot of arm work before she managed to stand up, only to take the chair with her, which required further combat, until she nearly fell backward. We doubled over laughing, and she knew she looked ridiculous.

"Silly boys. Come help your auntie out," she said.

That was our first impression of our auntie, but we quickly took to her, even though she could laugh your ear off. "If you don't hear me talking or laughing, I'm either sleeping or I'm dead," she would say.

She doted on the five of us, especially me.

Being a typical optimist, she never fretted over her bleak situation. The only exception was Yashu's marriage. But in a couple of weeks she was her old self again.

Auntie had adopted Yashu as a baby and treated her like her own cherished daughter. She wanted her to find a husband who would marry into the Chen family to continue the line. After high school, Yashu went to work and fell in love with a man from a family of devout Christians. Auntie would have objected even if he'd been willing to take Yashu's name, for to her, he was one of those "damned Christians."

The power of tradition had eroded over time, so this did not make Yashu a bad girl, and it was the only thing Auntie could find to complain about. They loved each other, and the man made many concessions, all of which Auntie rejected. Even Father's intervention could not change the girl's mind.

In the end, Yashu found courage in love. On one autumn day, she packed up a few changes of clothing and made a tearful journey alone from Luodong to Kaohsiung to get married. Before she left, Auntie locked herself in her room and refused to see her, though she was standing outside the door crying her heart out. Yashu berated herself and apologized over and over, making Father feel so bad he rushed after her to be her witness at the wedding without telling Auntie.

Five months went by, and a slight bulge was detectable under Yashu's loose dress. No longer a frivolous, childish girl, she now looked mature, a real mother-to-be, yet her eyes brimmed with endless sorrow and regret.

"When did Mr. Wu leave?" I asked.

"Yesterday. He'll come back for me in a few days."

"Did you write to your mother after you left?"

"I did. My husband often had me send gifts or money." She sighed. "But I never received a single word from her. I know she'll never forgive me."

Actually, Auntie talked about Yashu often after she left, sounding pleased about her filial acts.

I did my best to console Yashu until the incense burned down and we got ready to leave.

"You'll be a mother soon, Ah-shu," I said, drawing a bashful look from her. I continued with a lighthearted question: "What do you want, a boy or a girl?"

We were standing in front of the grave; she hesitated before saying, "I think—whatever she likes."

We held hands and bowed before walking off, but it didn't feel right to leave like that. So I offered my usual farewell phrase, the one I'd used when I'd gone to see her in the past: "We're going home now, Auntie."

This time she didn't reply with "Don't be in such a hurry. Stay and eat with us."

Yashu began to cry. I pressed my army cap down low, as two lines of hot tears burned their way down my cheek. I took her hand, and we walked off into a cold wind.

1963

A Man and His Pocketknife

Having taken his luggage back home the week before, Yangyu could keep his hands in his pockets as he walked onto the Taipei train station platform. He was squeezing a pocketknife sheath in the left one. *Father made a mistake in having me, a never-ending worry that's eating away at his heart,* he said to himself. *Mother, of course, knows nothing. Auntie has been nice to me recently, but what good does that do? What can they hope for from me? Worst of all, I have to make it back home today.*

Lost in thought, he mistakenly went to the No. 3 platform for Tamsui. Before he walked off, a man came up from behind and slapped him on the shoulder. "Going back to Tamsui, Old K?" Yangyu turned around. "I'm sorry," the man hastened to say, "I thought you were someone else." He vanished into the crowd. Looking at the ripple effects of the man pushing through the mass of humanity, Yangyu muttered to himself, *Oh, no. I'm going back to Luodong, thank you! I made a mistake, too.*

The platform clock told him that the train would not leave for another sixteen minutes, plenty of time for him to stroll to the

No. 2 platform. He went up the overhead walkway, sticking to the left side, right in the way of people rushing down the stairs like rocks rolling off a hill. Every one of them bumped into him. A few, young men like him, stopped to stare after the collision. He turned and smiled. "What's wrong? Think I was someone else?"

It was such a muggy day that the hand squeezing the pocketknife in his pocket was sweating. His thoughts returned to his parents. *They really shouldn't have had me. Why couldn't they have had a few more kids like Yangjun and Yangwu? They never went against out parents' wishes; they never rolled around on the ground, or put a toad in Mother's pocket and made her faint from fright. I was the only one for whom lying was as easy as molding clay, like the time I asked Father to give me ten NT to pay for the window I'd broken at school.* Yangyu continued with his train of thought. *They really shouldn't have had me. It was bad for them and it's bad for me. Worst of all, they need me to make it back home today.*

The train for Su-ao slowly backed up to the No. 2 platform, where the passengers returning to Lanyang area had never looked so anxious.

***

For most people who had moved away from home and wanted to return to Lanyang, the last local express from Taipei to Su-ao was their favorite. On this day, after a chance encounter, two young acquaintances sat across from each other in the last car. It was not so much a surprise meeting as it was abrupt and somewhat awkward.

It was the height of summer, and people were lightly dressed; exhaustion had claimed all the passengers. Most were lying back in their seats, while the men sitting by the windows had their feet raised as high as they could get them. A few were sitting up for murmured conversations.

"Married yet?" He wasn't dying to get a reply from her. They hadn't seen each other in two years.

"Yes."

"Really?"

"Really!"

"Happy?"

"Very," she said unhesitatingly. As she answered his questions, Xiumei stared at the blade in his left hand, with which he was deftly peeling a pear. She held her breath until the peel, which was nearly down to the floor, finally broke. Yangyu looked up and their eyes met, coming together with a clang. Whoever looked away first would suffer a blow to his or her self-esteem. As he swallowed and forced himself to hold his gaze, he saw her breasts rise and fall, so full they seemed about to burst through her nylon blouse. That reminded him of the night he'd laid his ear against her breast to capture the wondrous sound of her heart beating; he could recall the sound of that heart thumping against his eardrum.

"You haven't changed a bit," she said.

"How can you say that?" He did not want to admit that his self-esteem had suffered. The best strategy was to pretend, so he looked down to continue working on the now naked pear, its soft white flesh rolling out beneath his blade like wood shavings from a carpenter's plane. "You mean the knife?"

"You! Everything," she said, to his great delight.

"Everything?" He waved the knife in the air and smiled. He wanted to say something, but changed his mind.

They fell silent for a while. She kept her eyes on his hands until the pear was gone. His left hand and the blade had always worked well together. Now he wanted to know the truth, even if it no longer mattered to him, so he asked with a sense of fervor: "Married?"

"Married."

"Really?"

"Really!"

"No lie?"

"No lie!"

"Your answers are so boring." He was disappointed by her responses.

"I got married last year while you were completing your military service."

"Oh! You've got me wrong, madam. I believe everything you say. I was just saying that the way you answered by repeating my question was boring."

"Your questions were boring, too."

The train entered the Sandiaoling tunnel, accentuating the sound of wheels crunching on the tracks. People who were talking either stopped or raised their voices.

"Boring, mechanical, like the sound of the train. Listen: Married? Married! Chug-chug. Really? Really! Chug-chug." That made them laugh. But then silence returned, as if they felt they shouldn't have laughed.

"Married—" He cut through the folded evening paper, a meaningless act, but he couldn't resist. "Marriage must mean something different to us. If not, we would have been thought of as married long ago."

Xiumei wasn't bothered by the mockery; she was convinced that he still loved her, that he had always been serious about their relationship. Later, she would think fondly of him whenever she had a spat with her husband, recalling the way he had mocked her for getting married, and regretting her decision to do so; she would feel her heart stir.

"Let's not talk about the past," Xiumei said. "What are your plans now that you've fulfilled your military obligation?"

"To get married!"

The conductor was outraged when he saw the fruit peel and trash under Yangyu's seat, and glared at him as he came down the aisle checking tickets.

The newspaper had now been shredded into a pile of unsettling strips.

Even with an hour to go, Yangyu sensed that time was passing too fast, and he had never felt so awful about his family as he did at that moment. With whatever time was left, he wanted to find something else to slice with his blade; his fingernails were would work if nothing else was available. It had been a long time since he'd used scissors or nail clippers. With the pocketknife, he could trim his nails as neatly as if he were using nail clippers. No matter how late it was when he reached home at night, he sharpened his knife blade, not going to bed until it had parted a hair he had laid atop it and blown on.

The train went through a series of tunnels. Yangyu and Xiumei were both thinking quietly about their first exchange, which resembled the monotonous sound of the train's wheels on the tracks—Married? Married! Really? Really! Happy? Very!

***

The train glided along unhurriedly. A blind old man who had obviously been away for many years grew excited when he detected in the crosscurrent the fragrant smell of cypress logs brought down from Mount Taiping. He shook the boy beside him and shouted, "We're back in our Luodong!" His cheek muscles danced happily. Many of the passengers stuck their heads out, searching hungrily for familiar faces in the crowd waiting behind the platform gate. Shouts from over there and calls from over here created a warm, congenial scene of chaos.

As if they hadn't yet reached their destination, Yangyu and Xiumei leaned quietly against their seat backs. He, in particular, was in no hurry, wanting to linger as long as possible on the train. In the meantime, the Luodong passengers looked ridiculous to him, seemingly so eager to get off they would have jumped out the window if they could.

"No one's here to meet you?" he asked.

"He's in Taipei. And you?"

"Me?" Yangyu sneered. "No one will be waiting for me, especially not my family. I came back for a few days last week." His facial muscles twitched from a chill rising from deep inside.

"From Kaohsiung?"

"Of course!"

"What's so urgent that you have to make the trip twice in a week?" She paused. "To get married?"

"You women have a nose for matters like that. You guessed right." His tone was cold and sharp, like the blade in his hand.

They remained on the platform talking until the other passengers had all left. They then headed to the gate; the ticket collector frowned when Yangyu handed him a ticket trimmed by his blade, and continued to stare at their backs before turning off the lights and plunging the plaza into darkness. Yangyu and Xiumei turned back at the same time and saw the digital clock atop the station entrance.

"Wow, it's almost midnight. I'm exhausted from riding trains, so I won't walk you home. Besides—"

"Besides what? Besides! I know what you were going to say." She looked peeved.

"I'm glad you understand. It's not the same between us now, you know."

Several pedicab drivers pedaled up to them.

"Want to take one?" he asked.

"No. Let's walk and talk. I'll see you home." She continued when he didn't object, "Let's walk by the river."

"Whatever." He paused. "There's something different about you. Maybe it's the weather? It's so hot."

"Too hot for you?"

"It is. Very uncomfortable."

An old path ran alongside the river; everything looked the same, all but the willows, which were taller than when they'd walked together two years before. As a sky full of stars covered the surface of the murmuring river, flickering and shimmering like their many memories, Yangyu reached out to pluck a willow twig and began whittling it.

"One day I followed you all the way to the library from here after seeing willow shavings on the ground."

Yangyu did not respond. He had been as silent as the knife in his hand since they'd turned off the street from the station. On this late starlit night his knife emitted a quiet, cold blue glint, creating a new and very strange feeling. At that moment, he could sense a force compressing the air around them. What an audacious woman, he said to himself. *Where did she get the courage to walk down an eerie road so late at night with a crazy man wielding a sharp pocketknife? She's got nerve, being with a deranged man, a man with a lethal knife.*

"What's wrong? Are you in hurry to get home?" Xiumei eyed him curiously.

"Why do you ask?"

"You've started walking really fast."

"Oh, no reason. I think it's the heat. Strange there's not even a breeze tonight." He began to whistle, a raspy sound, and slowed down his pace.

"That sounds terrible."

"But it's what we need to do. When I was a kid, my grandma told me to whistle like that to get a breeze going." He paused. "See—feel the breeze?"

"Nonsense! My grandpa said whistling at night summons ghosts."

"If your grandpa had married my grandma, they'd have fought every day. People of their generation wouldn't dare get a divorce." He was pleased with his comment, but his laugh seemed vacuous to her. He'd been laughing in that strange way the whole time. But he turned serious and said, "What would our friends say if they saw us together like this?" The knife lay in his left hand.

"No idea. But there's no one here."

No one! His heart skipped a beat. A woman and a man with a knife in his sweaty palm walking down an eerie road beside a river late at night. The stilled knife made his hand itch for something to destroy; a heavy object was swelling in his chest, and nearly driving him mad. He knew what would happen if he said no to his father tonight. They had given him time to think it over, but he knew what he was going to tell them.

He spotted a tin can up ahead and kicked it, startling a dog on the other side of a fence. Gripping the knife tightly, he quickened his pace again, leaving Xiumei behind.

"Yangyu," she called out breathlessly. "What's wrong with you, Yangyu? Wait up."

Her shout so panicked him that he took off running. Hampered by her high heels, she decided to quit chasing him. After a moment, he turned and shouted, "Stay back, Xiumei! Go home! It's not safe here." He started running again.

Starlight shimmered in the sky. The water in the river rippled, but the croaking of the frogs stopped. There wasn't the hint of a breeze in the air.

***

"We thought you weren't coming back today. The last train came in over an hour ago. Where were you?" Auntie said as she bolted the door. "Your father's not in a good mood, so watch what you say."

"But I have to say what's on my mind." He relented when he saw her wounded look. "I'll be careful."

"Why don't you say yes?" She looked at him expectantly.

"I can't."

A gecko that must have recently moved in behind the clock scrambled out and plastered itself on the wall as the aging clock struck midnight. After three or four bells, however, the lizard could tell it didn't have to worry about the noise, any more than it did about the sound of footsteps or doors closing. But the false alarm had clearly caused enough panic for its translucent belly to heave violently. Naturally, Yangyu's father noticed the gecko when he looked up at the clock and knew that his chest must be heaving as fiercely as the gecko's. He told himself not to lose his temper or rail at the boy again, no matter what. Then there might be hope.

"You're back." The father said when Yangyu walked in. "Go get something to eat, and we'll talk later."

"There's food in the pot," Auntie said. "I'll bring it in."

"No need. I'll go get some noodles." His father left despite Yangyu's objection. Yangyu felt terrible, wishing it could be like it was before, when his father was preoccupied with his business and ignored the children, giving him a beating with no explanation when he was angry.

"Dad has changed. He's like a total stranger," Yangyu said anxiously.

"Yes, so you must think about what he wants and not cause him any pain. See how he doesn't even care about dignity anymore?"

"That's not my fault. Things kept getting worse, that's all."

"We've been through this already. You must admit that Ah-yu is a good girl and quite pretty. If you marry her, you'll not only have a good wife, but you'll help take care of your father's debt, and we'll get to keep the house—"

"I know all that," Yangyu cut her off. "But I can't do it. Please don't talk like him."

"I may be your stepmother, but I want more than he does—" She began to cry.

His father came in, followed by a boy from the noodle stand carrying a plate of food and a bowl of soup. Yangyu felt sorry for his father, who would do anything, except die, for his children. He had never been so placid, like tilled soil. But he abruptly changed his mind about his father, who now seemed devious and contemptible; he resented the burden of conscience caused by his father's pitiful and despicable behavior. *I can't die,* he vowed to himself. *It's toxic to devour Father's dignity. I can't eat it. Absolutely not.* Without being aware of it, he took out his pocketknife to whittle the chopsticks.

"Have some noodles," his father said.

"I'm not hungry." Yangyu looked irritated; he loathed his father's phony act. "What are you doing, Dad? Don't treat me like this. I—I can't stand it. Just go ahead and say what you want to say to me." Agitated now, he pressed the blade down on the chopstick and cut off a large chunk.

"I just want to say it's great that you're back." Father forced himself to remain calm. "We can revive our family prosperity. I want to start a business, and I'm happy you're back."

"No. That's not what you want to say. You're not telling the truth." The steam from the noodles and soup had dissipated. Yangyu picked up the other chopstick and began slicing. They fell silent, which made the house feel as if a bomb could go off at any moment. None of them could stand the stillness. Someone had to say something, no matter what might happen next; they all felt it was time to speak their minds. Yangyu cleaved what was left of the chopstick into halves.

"I can't change. I just can't." He moved on to slicing the edge of the table. "I must have a say in my marriage. A happy couple is supposed to have everyone's good wishes. I'm the most important one in this matter. Why don't you treat me like before and let me live or die on my own?" He felt much better now. Father was unusually composed, which surprised and disappointed Yangyu at the same time, for he wanted to leave this confined, stifling space as soon as possible. His father's gaze was locked on the knife in his hand as it smoothed a corner of the table, bit by bit.

Father finally spoke up, after a prolonged, terrifying silence. "I will only listen to you this one time. You decide: either you do what I want and marry her or I die." He said this calmly. Yangyu did not respond; he just kept carving the table. Auntie couldn't hold back. "Nonsense! That's nonsense. Don't say things like that." She had been crying the whole time.

"I can't stand it. Say something. Tell me what you want." His father was getting more worked up by the minute, but Yangyu continued carving the table, keeping his head down.

"Speak up! Damn you!" Father's shout startled him, but not enough to make him stop carrying on with his old affliction.

Yangyu's agitation showed in the increased speed of his carving. That irked his father more than anything. To him, the pocketknife was to blame for everything. Without warning, he rushed Yangyu like a madman, grabbing his son's left hand and shouting at the top of his lungs, "Give it to me! I'm going to throw it away!" "No," Yangyu said. "Never!" Auntie rushed over and fell on her knees to hold her husband around the waist, crying and shouting at the same time. They didn't have to shout anymore, but continued to spit out every word. *"Give it to me. I'm going to get rid of it tonight."* "*No, never.*" Neither would give in, and both were panting heavily. "You, must, get, married," Father sputtered as he tried to snatch the knife away. "No, I won't." Yangyu struggled to catch his breath. "Even if she's willing and agrees to suffer with me, I wouldn't want to give her the white rose of sorrow. How crazy would that be!" They were fighting for the knife the whole time they kept up the exchange. "I'm saying my pain is a flower, a thoughtful, noble—" Father tried but failed to take the knife away as Yangyu was talking. "*You!*" They were breathing even harder now. "That—all that talk about nobility, it's ridiculous. A noble white rose!" Yangyu snapped. "You're crazy! Hey!" They rammed each other and tangled into a heap, knocking over chairs and the table. Yangyu struggled free when his father was distracted by his stepmother's ear-piercingly shrill cries, but in the process he opened a large gash on his right arm, and harsh-looking blood poured out like water from a spring. Yangyu said softly to his father, who looked somewhat guilty, "Happy now?"

At that moment, everything seemed far, far away from the bleeding arm, the men's raspy breathing, and the woman's tears.

***

Yangyu was only in the third grade at the time.

He went alone to the empty lot behind the lumberyard one day after school was out; he wanted to see where he'd buried a sparrow the day before. Two sixth-graders fighting when he got there. The bigger boy, who had a harelip, was sitting astride the smaller, skinnier one, landing punch after punch on his weaker opponent, who could only put up ineffectual, symbolic resistance. Yangyu was horrified. He wanted to help the poor boy out, but he could only tremble at the sight; he felt like crying, but no sound emerged. Some workers who had come to move logs were enjoying the scene and cheering the boys on instead of stopping the fight. Standing in the circle around them, a couple of the men even instructed the boy on the bottom how to get on top, which he tried to do by scissoring the other boy with his legs. But the bigger kid used that moment to push his opponent's face into the ground and pin him. Yangyu began to sob softly. One of the workers asked him, "*Is that your brother?*" When Yangyu didn't answer him, he turned and shouted, "Stop! Stop fighting! Your kid brother is crying." The man walked over and picked the harelipped boy up with one hand; the other workers laughed as they walked off with their logs. After picking up his pencil box and its contents, the bigger boy looked around and muttered, "Where's my pocketknife?" When he couldn't find it, he went home. Yangyu bashfully looked at the other boy, who was eyeing him, a kid who had admitted to being the younger brother of a complete stranger. Yangyu turned his face to dry his tears as he walked away. The boy also walked off. But after a few steps, Yangyu spotted an object on the ground—a four-inch-long pocketknife in a sheath, obviously the one the hare lipped boy had been looking for. Out of disgust for its owner, he decided he'd throw it into the toilet. He picked it up to examine it closely; it was fairly new and very sharp. So he took it with him to check on the dead sparrow. To his delight, the blade came in handy for digging around the bird. He'd always wanted a knife, but his mother had told him it was dangerous for a little boy to own one. He was happy to finally have one.

It did not take long to dig up the dead bird, but his mood quickly soured. The dead sparrow's eyes were sunken, and maggots were crawling in and out. Above him the sun was a sweltering ball of fire, while the odor of decomposing flesh permeated the air around him. With a heavy heart, he reburied the bird, found a brick, and put it on the spot. It would serve as a tombstone, but required an inscription, as he recalled his mother's name on her stone. He unsheathed the knife to make a presentable tombstone for the bird, carving on the brick an image that looked to him like a bird, with unusually big eyes and beak. He left then, but came back after only a few steps to look at the marker. He'd left out the bird's feet, so he added them before finally heading home. His mind was preoccupied on his way home—he hated the boy with the harelip and the workers; he was bashful; he thought about the dead sparrow and how it had looked when it was alive. A living sparrow can sing, but a dead one has maggots in its eyes. There must have been maggots in Mother's eyes, too, and that was called death. Why did Mother, who had often told him stories, have to end up like that? What does somebody have to do to stay alive?

He thought about the pocketknife, a nice thing to have. *I could murder a bad guy, sharpen my pencils, kill a snake, and carve something with this.* He spotted a chinaberry tree and walked over to try the blade on the bark. After carving his name, he added a picture of a bird, remembering the feet this time. Little by little, his mind cleared of everything but the knife.

He did not want to run into the boy with the harelip, who might ask him about his pocketknife. But at the end of summer the boy graduated, and Yangyu could take the knife out openly to sharpen pencils for other kids, carve more birds on trees, and leave his name on his desk and chair. Many kids on campus were envious, and that made him happy. He was punished at school several times and scolded by his father over the knife, but that only made his fondness for it grow. After a few years, he became adept at carving many more images. He found uses for his knife every day through middle school and high school, and later when he attended college through work-study and in the military. Whenever his hands were free, he would take it out to whittle twigs, carve tree bark, cut up paper, and trim his nails. The concave curve of the blade lessened over time, but it was an authentic Shilin pocketknife made in Taiwan, sometimes called an Eight Sages knife. The blade was made of top-quality steel, and the more it was honed, the sharper it got. By now it had become part of him. The knife did not affect his emotional state when he carried it, but his equilibrium would have suffered if he'd lost it. He kept the blade sharp at all times; his eyes grew to be like the knife, and he felt like cutting whatever and whoever he fixed his gaze on.

***

Yangyu agreed to teach civic education at his alma mater after the family property was liquidated and his father asked a friend to talk to him. "Don't let the old folks down again. There's nothing wrong with teaching civic education just because you graduated first in your class in water resources engineering. It's so much better than someone with a degree in home economics teaching English at school during the day and tutoring in English at night."

The knife got more use after he started his teaching job, as he found more to carve, including the chalk box.

"I think you're being foolish. Why did you have to argue with the Old Cat? Since you can't change society, you have to adapt to it," his college friend Lin said to him one day. Yangyu had finally asked the principal to let him teach algebra, which had led to a terrible row. Yangyu ran to the gym equipment room to be alone. "Everyone knows you didn't ask to teach algebra so you could some extra money in the after-school sessions, but the Old Cat needs that money to buy stinky fish to feed his kittens at home."

Yangyu did not reply as he angrily cut away on the object in his hands.

"Don't cut up the chalk box! You'll be in trouble if the Old Cat finds out."

"So what? This is not a chalk box." He cut into it with a vengeance.

"Not a chalk box? Ah, then it's the Old Cat! Ha-ha!" Lin laughed smugly. "I see that now. Sometimes you take all of society in your hand to cut up, shred, or completely destroy."

"I'd like to be alone," Yangyu said crankily.

"I have a class. I'm afraid you might want to cut me up, too. I just hope I'm not a chalk box." Lin walked off.

Sitting on a gym mat, Yangyu felt that he was finally able to look at himself objectively. Focusing on everything that made him unhappy, he dissected, judged, and condemned with his eyes and his knife, discovering a different dominion for himself and the knife, a realization born of reflections on the past. Indeed, he'd go for his knife whenever he felt outraged or indignant. He wondered why that hadn't dawned on him until now. A sudden sadness rose up inside him, and he said to himself, *The worst tragedy for humans is being able to see oneself clearly. Humans launch themselves into an infinite pursuit of perfection so no one will dare to take a closer look at themselves. Who would want to face one's own repulsiveness and ignorance?* He was reminded of the fairy tale in which a queen ordered all the mirrors destroyed in her country because she was afraid of looking old.

Without really knowing what he was doing, he stood up and began cutting one of the parallel bars. Lin returned after his class.

"What are you doing?" he asked. "Am I the parallel bars now?"

Yangyu was taken aback. "No! I am."

"Why?"

"I have to conquer myself before I triumph over others."

"What good does that kind of thinking do?"

"Here's what I'm thinking," Yangyu continued. "Sometimes a thought, or an idea, materializes like an uninvited guest who stays for a while and then leaves. Try as we might, we can't remember his face." He continued to cut off pieces as he waited for Lin's reply.

"Your knife is keeping things from remaining in your head."

"Let's not talk about this anymore. Neither of us is a philosopher, so we're wasting our time without any possibility of finding an answer. What's going on with the Old Cat?"

"He's still talking to the curriculum dean, about you, of course. You might want to start looking for another job for next semester."

"The Old Cat asked me a ridiculous question when I first came.

He asked what I had been doing before the military service. I told him I was preparing for the military service." Yangyu laughed. "I think I left an unfavorable impression."

"Your mouth is a knife, too."

***

Yangyu found another teaching job at B Middle School. "Why don't you teach civic education," the principal asked him, "since you have experience in the subject?" Before that, Yangyu had gone for an interview at D Girls' Middle School, where the aging principal said, "It won't work for us here, because you're young and single." So he would start teaching civic education at B Middle School when the summer break was over.

By the time summer break was half over, the blade had narrowed considerably, but he continued to sharpen it. Time seemed to pass slowly, and each day was longer than the one before. He felt suffocated by the air around him and annoyed by a singsong melody from the Anhui area that was continually being played in his neighborhood. He had to go out for some fresh air, but where? At the bus depot, he hit upon the idea of going to the port town.

As he fingered the knife in his pocket, he looked out the window and read the names of the shops until the bus left town. He shut his eyes and saw a group of listless students dozing off in his civic education class. *I'd do the same if I were them,* he said to himself. Then he heard his father cough. *Father made a mistake in having me, and it didn't do him or me any good.* An image of lips like rose petals emerged in his head. He shifted his body and said, "toad." His mind wandered; at one point he wanted to recall his mother's face, but the memory was too hazy. Still with his eyes shut, he tried to push away the confusing fog caused by his effort to remember her. Someone pulled the cord and the bus stopped. "No, not yet," the passenger said after taking a look. "I'll get off, then," Yangyu said. "Where are we?" "Chushuikou," the conductress replied. He got off, trailed by laughter from the others on the bus.

The bus rounded a corner at the foothills. Without the annoying noise, Yangyu felt alone in a different world. The ocean was to the east of the highway, across from the rice field and beyond the beefwood windbreak. To the west, at the edge of the sweet potato field, was a mountain range. Not far from where he had gotten off, a path stretched out from the mountains, like a welcome mat, and he decided to go up into the mountains. First he dug up a large sweet potato so that he could have something to cut as he walked. When he was done with that, he snapped off a branch from a roadside cassia tree. Later he veered off the path and climbed to a higher spot, where he took out that day's newspaper and leaned against a cassia tree by a boulder. He forced himself to read, but could only manage a few personal ads before he rolled it up and began cutting. After a few tries, he decided that the blade needed sharpening, so he spat on the boulder, but his spit was quickly absorbed by the thirsty rock. A change in method was required; he spread the paper on the ground so he could slice the page open. The same questions cropped up in his head, but with the difference that he had come here specifically to think about them.

Why do I suffer? he asked himself. *Because I'm alive. Does that mean every living person suffers? Maybe, except some don't realize it. Could all living creatures be endowed with an instinct to fear death, in order to protect and safeguard their suffering? What's the price? Hmm, I seem to be on the right track. Let me keep at it.* He continued to slice away at the paper on the ground.

In my view, our animal instinct to fear death derives from the will to protect our lives. I'm human, so I can only talk about how I feel as a human. Our will to live is related to self-preservation. But what kind of self is that? An independent, normal self. But isn't that too vague? Doesn't it sound anarchistic? Ah, that's too far-fetched. Let's take, for example, a harnessed mule that turns round and round in a dark mill, utterly devoid of hope. That's easy to understand: it's happy as long as you give it enough to eat when it's hungry and a mate when it's ready. But not humans. We humans want to push the millstone our own way; but the average person can't have a normal self before he has an absolute guarantee that all of his basic needs will be met. The core of the problem is accomplishing both at the same time, which is why many people suffer so much they want to die. Based on this conclusion, God has the last laugh. I don't believe in anything. But I would be envious if such reasoning meant that God is omnipotent.

By that point the paper was a mess, crisscrossed with cuts. Yangyu turned to the cassia tree and carved the image of a sparrow on it before getting down on his knees and carefully carving his name, followed by the date. His mind was busier than the knife in his hand.

"Hey, Yangyu." He didn't turn his head, knowing full well that he was alone. "Hey, Yangyu. You say that many people want to die, so why don't they?" It was hot and his face was bathed in sweat. "Aren't you one of those who want to die?"

"Yes, I've thought of it."

"That answer isn't good enough for me. You left out half of the question."

"These people, myself included, of course, are tethered by a flimsy thread. They will die once the thread is broken."

"What does it represent?"

"Maybe a shred of hope or maybe ignorance; it could be a lack of courage or a sense of responsibility."

"So what kind of thread is the one tied to you?"

"I'd like to hear Beethoven's music and read Sartre's later works a few more times."

"The sparrow you carved today is your best ever."

He smiled proudly.

"Why do you like this one?"

"I don't know. I think about it whenever I feel like carving something."

"That's the self, too."

"I agree with you completely." Yangyu was pleased. He rested against the tree after looking at the image and the words he had carved. With nothing to do, he felt a tremor in his knife-wielding hand, which was unsettling.

"What's wrong, Yangyu? Why do you look unhappy?"

"Hey!" He sat up. "I've uncovered a secret. Humans aren't afraid of dying; they just fear the pain before death. I think many people would want to die right away if someone invented a method or drug for a painless death."

"And a fearless death as well."

"That's important, too."

"Do you want to die now? No more Beethoven or Sartre?"

"They're too expensive for me." He started trimming his nails.

"What song would you sing before you died?"

Yangyu began singing, but he couldn't finish because he had started too high.

Looking to the east for the ocean's embrace
A wild, boundless fertile land
Gazing up at the west for the mountains' beauty

Encircling three sides in the distance.

"What kind of song is that? It sounds like a squealing sow."

"My middle school's song."

"Do you miss the place?"

"No! I was expelled. I was the first student they ever expelled."

"You hated it, then?"

"I don't know." He was tearing up.

"Were you a terrible student?"

"I don't know. All I did was go to the bulletin board and tear off the list of students who were required to take a makeup exam."

"Why did you do that?"

"I didn't want Lan to see my name. I had just written her a letter the day before, and I needed a reply, so she couldn't know I had to take a makeup exam."

"Then you left home and attended one school after another, is that right?"

"Why did none of the schools like a student like me?"

"Let's change the subject. Who would you pick if I asked you to think of someone?"

"My mother." Yangyu paused. "She died when I was in the second grade."

"What do you recall about her?"

"Nothing. But I would likely be a different person if she were still alive."

"You think so?"

"I do when I'm suffering."

"What about the next person?"

"The first woman I bought."

"Was she pretty?"

"No. I don't remember anything about her."

"Was she able to satisfy you?"

"Not at all. I think she was ten years older than I was, at least."

"Then why do you still remember her? Especially now?"

"That's funny, isn't it? I was just reminded of her. I paid her double."

"Why did you do that? Did she give you something else?"

"I really don't know why. I happened to have sixty NT on me, I guess."

"What reminded you of her?"

"I left my underwear at her place. It made me mad because I'd just bought it two days earlier."

"That's hilarious."

Yangyu laughed and said, "It would be nice if dying could be that interesting and hilarious."

"What do you think would make for a painless death?"

"Like with this knife." Yangyu laid the blade against his wrist. "It would hurt a lot if I cut it very slowly," he said as he gestured. "But if I were to slit it like this …" He slashed his wrist, without knowing why. "Oh! I really did it. I actually slit it." Terror-stricken, he put down the knife to press his left hand on the cut, but warm, wet blood was already gushing out. He panicked and ran down the slope. The sun spun before his eyes, so did the trees and everything else, followed by a hazy fog in his head, and then nothing.

***

Three days later, the first woodcutter to go up the mountain found the young man's body by a boulder and a cassia tree. By then the eyes were sunken, and maggots were crawling in and out, busy at work. His left hand was still clutching a rusty pocketknife.

1965

Follow My Feet

On the day before Typhoon Betty hit, the sun was still blistering hot in the afternoon. The radio station's typhoon warning was inserted into the three-hour radio slot devoted to popular songs, creating a halfhearted audience among the residents on this street in Yilan, a city that had frequently suffered the most damage from storms in recent years.

Once again, my feet moved along the street. I was in desperate need of some cold water, a thought that entered my head when I spotted some drinking glasses in a shaved-ice shop's display case with an intriguing but simple blue fish design. The fish looked relaxed and happy. *They'll come to life once the glasses are filled with water,* I said to myself, as I experienced a rare moment of cheer. In fact, my buoyed spirit was only an impromptu of the heart, since a bad mood had been the norm for me over the past month.

"Say, what do you sell in these glasses?" I asked the girl who called every young man doing military service *gege*, older brother. I'd often heard her do that when I walked by.

"Either papaya or guava juice." I figured that the radio must be playing one of her favorite songs, because she was not making me feel welcome with her head buried in some sheet music. But I didn't care about that. I was convinced, from her reply, that the fish would surely die of suffocation if the glasses were filled with a thick, opaque liquid like papaya or guava juice. So with a frown, I asked, "Can you put lemonade in it?" I don't like lemonade, actually. Did I feel sorry for the fish? Or did I want to see them come alive? I couldn't say.

"Sure." She used as little time as possible to take her eyes off the lyrics to glance my way.

"I'll have a glass of lemonade, then. Not too much lemon, and, oh, turn down the volume on the radio." I sat down at a table by the far wall. Before she brought my order, I tried to visualize the happy fish in a glass of lemonade. Two of them looked like they were kissing, reminding me of G and me. The girl brought the glass and set it down so that the fish were facing me. I didn't touch it. Resting my head on my folded arms, I moved my face up close to the glass, imagining that the bigger fish to the right was me and the small one was G. After a while, they seemed to grow bigger, but blurry. Droplets of condensation slid down the glass. Sunlight falling on the asphalt outside looked strangely hazy through the liquid and the glass. I stirred the contents with a straw, a maneuver that did not require moving my head. The ice cubes appeared to change shape, making me feel a sense of loss. In this unfamiliar visual field, what I needed most was to hear something that sounded familiar. The ice cubes clinked to create a silvery sound, a bit like G's happy laughter. She hadn't laughed like that for a while, at least not over the past month.

"I understand the torment you're suffering." My fiancée could offer only that simple phrase to comfort me after nearly a month of contemplation. Even she could tell it was a feeble gesture, though nothing else seemed appropriate. She added, "You don't have to be in a hurry to find another job. I was proud of you when you quit the newspaper. I admire how you loathe people who can't stand up for themselves and who stay in a job that rubs against their ideals."

In fact, I understood perfectly why she said that—anxiety brought on by my suffering and angst. I also knew she needed my support now more than ever, and that she would perk up the moment my mood lifted. What saddened me most, however, was how her emotional state was dictated by my honesty to myself, though I never meant to hurt her. My conflicting senses of duty and self magnified the heartache. Like someone at a fork in the road, I was forced to pick one route without being given enough time to consider my options. Worse yet, I realized that I'd reached that point after traveling a great distance over a dense and complex grid. I had to choose one of two abhorrent routes; I could not go back, even had there been a road for me to do so. That was the moment I truly felt the existence of time, which pushed me forward with a force that came from all the images it created. This must be what cruelty is like, a worst-case scenario; I had no time to ponder, which was the same as losing the ability to think. I realized that once I took the irreversible step forward to affirm myself, I could not simultaneously go backward to negate myself. I could lose my self-awareness or abandon myself to despair. I could not deceive myself just to make her happy. This was an ethical issue. So I said, "No, you can't understand the agony I'm experiencing."

She looked at me with surprise, and her hand slid off my shoulder. So I continued: "This has nothing to do with our love. Like you, I don't doubt that love for a moment."

"Could I have been blind when I fell for you?" she asked in tremulous voice.

"Didn't I just say it has nothing to do with our love?"

"Maybe we don't know each other well enough."

"We've done our best, and we'll never stop trying."

"I don't know what you mean by that." She looked perplexed.

"I don't always understand myself, either. But that's not uncommon," I added. "Are you absolutely sure about yourself?"

She considered my question but did not offer an answer. I continued: "Sometimes I'm afraid to think about myself. I try to dodge that self-persecuting thought whenever it comes up. Then I hit upon the ideal solution, which is to revile myself as much as possible, as if I were someone else." I realized she could easily misunderstand and misinterpret what I was saying, but I could not stop.

"That's awfully deep. I don't know what a self-persecuting thought is, so I have no idea what you're talking about." She looked downcast. "And I don't want to know. The only thing I can come up with is that you need to reflect on your suffering."

She began to sob, typical of a girl from an old-fashioned family. Her face was even more lovely when it was wet with tears. I seldom got to see her cry, most likely because we were so happy together. Except for one night, when she had thrown herself into my arms the moment she saw me. "I want to die," she had cried. "My father won't let me marry you, and I don't have the courage to fight him.

But I can't find the courage to leave you, either. So I want to die."

She was sobbing now. I wrapped my arms around her and kissed away her tears. The subtle salty taste melted away the knot of pain that had been inside me for so long, though it was only a momentary interlude in which I could forget myself and focus on her happiness.

My lips touched the glass; it was like kissing teardrops rolling down her cheeks.

"I do love you, Glakis." With my arms tightly around her, I felt my body dance as it sensed the happiness in her life since she had shed her sorrow.

After a prolonged silence, she said, "We're engaged to be married next month, but I have yet to hear you propose to me." She placed her hand over my mouth, as if she knew what I would say. "Later, when you feel like it."

"I feel like I've done it already."

"But you haven't said it."

"Is it that important?"

"I just want it to be more complete." She immediately corrected herself, "To be perfect."

"I can imagine how much this means to a girl. Unlike other expressions, it is a phrase that will continue to live in your heart."

She reached out again when she thought I was about to propose. Pinching my lips together, she repeated, "Later. It will come out naturally when you feel the need to say it."

I tried to say something, but she pinched my lips harder. It tickled me to think of my ridiculous lips looking like a duck's bill.

I grabbed a pen and a piece of paper and wrote, *Marry me, dear G! Even if my mouth looks like a duck's bill.*

She let go of my lips to snatch the pen and paper, and wrote with a smile, *Stupid duck! I should have put you in a cage.*

We carried on with our game of writing to each other until I could tell she was happy again. I reached back and switched off the lamp. The room turned dark; we had no use for light.

***

Sunlight fell lifelessly on the asphalt, where it remained immobilized. The glass had lost its brilliance, and I could no longer hear G's laughter as I stirred its contents. I looked up and saw the girl whispering to a friend, which made me suspect that they were talking about me. They must be, for they exchanged a look and stopped talking. Moving the straw closer, I took a sip, my eyes on the girl the whole time. In addition to my displeasure at their furtive behavior, the bitter, harsh taste of the lemonade soured my mood. To avoid talking to her, I checked the price list on the wall, took out three coins, and tossed them on the table before walking out—reluctantly. Somehow I felt slighted, and would have liked to smash something or pick a fight with someone, anyone. How about the programming director? No, too old. I'll leave it up to him whether he lives or dies. How about Ye, or the guy from Xiamen? A number of people who deserved a good beating came to mind—a selfish, devious, manipulative, snobbish bunch. I was sure I could teach them a lesson, but one of them was about to become a father, while the others were too small and frail. I hated the fact that they were no match for me, for if they had been, I wouldn't have felt that my self-worth would be diminished if I picked a fight with them. I really wanted to beat them up, an urge that made my heart race and my face burn. Walking down the street, I vowed to strike out at anyone who bumped into me and did not apologize. But, in fact, a part of me did not want to run into any of them or pick a fight to boost my self-esteem, so I avoided places that might lead to an encounter. I wasn't afraid of them, no, that wasn't it. I just didn't want to run into them. So I guess I was afraid of them after all.

Dark clouds blocking the sun were blown away by first gusts of the typhoon winds, but patchy clouds were forming over the Pacific and being pushed this way, even though they themselves were oblivious, as if asleep. The wind was blowing hard up there, though no breeze stirred down here; so when the sun came out, I saw many faces that were suffering in the stifling heat.

Without realizing it, I had arrived at the station, where a train heading to Su-ao had just left. Peace and quiet returned to the station after the commotion. Only a few passengers were sitting or lying on the bench in the spacious waiting room, looking like lifeless objects, except for a pair of beggars, one older and one younger, who were busy counting coins. With a crisp clink, they laid them out on the bench. I saw the young man jerk his hand back after it was slapped. The old beggar glanced at me while saying something to the young one. A cool breeze made me look up at the fan above; I decided to sit down.

Self-persecuting thoughts refer to a state, a terrifying, searing pain, G. It doesn't have a specific definition. For instance, you have ideals. No, that won't work. For example, you have a conscience and you'd like to follow it to do good, but circumstances won't allow that. You will run into trouble in life if you don't obey the dictates of your surroundings, but you will reproach yourself if you do. You will be persecuting yourself if you think about whether or not to be true to your conscience and your ideals.

I wish I had explained that to her, though she had said I didn't have to. The young beggar walked up at some point, bobbing his head mechanically the whole time. I looked over at the old beggar, who looked away. Just as I was about to reach into my pocket for some change, the young man walked off looking disappointed. I felt sorry, but I didn't want to call him back. What an improbable miscommunication. On top of my earlier distress, I was now tormented by the pain of being misunderstood. People's laziness and overconfidence disgusts me. The young beggar should have stayed a moment longer before walking off disappointed. *He should have at least done that for me*, I said to myself.

The station was getting crowded again, forcing a man lying on the bench to sit up and relinquish part of the seat. With his feet up on the bench and his arms around his legs, he was able to lay his head down on his knees to resume his nap. The beggars went into action again, but skipped me and held their hands out to a woman beside me, making the departing passengers on both sides look at me curiously. I returned their gaze with an unfriendly look; they turned and looked straight ahead, calm and composed, as if they knew why the beggars had skipped me. I thought I should have the right to slap them. I was incensed.

Four people in conspicuous dress arrived when the waiting room was near capacity: two middle-aged women, plus a girl and a man. Over their street clothes, they had on sleeveless, collarless sack-like white vests with bright red words stitched on the front and back—*Jesus Loves You* and *I'm a Sinner*. They passed out flyers, and I was upset when I saw them skip the two beggars, so I pretended not to see it when a flyer was thrust at me. My thoughts turned to religion.

I was with Ju before I met G. She pushed Jesus on me as if he were some kind of merchandise. Once I went to church with her to listen to Pastor Lei's sermon. He said we were all sinners and that God would pay for my repentance with his son's blood.

I told her I'd rather be a sinner forever than suffer in church to be sin-free. She was hurt at first, but later she lied to her family about going to church when she actually went with me into the fields, where we used the Bible as a pillow. Ju was a beautiful girl, but unbearably shallow. I began to loathe religion after being with her. To me, all religions use despicable means to instill faith into their followers; they seize on people's weakness and resort to threats, abduction, and other immoral ruses. Imagine a group of mindless followers on a cruise ship being tricked into going to the railing to watch a whale spew water out of its blowhole. They are all pushed overboard when their attention is on the wondrous sight, so no one gets a look at the would-be killer's face. As they flail their arms for help in the water, all these poor victims can see is a kind-looking man (who is actually their victimizer) tossing in lifesavers. They are tearfully grateful to him.

I watched as the four self-professed sinners, who stood out among the crowd, talked and laughed on the steps at the entrance when they were satisfied with a job well done. Their presence jarred with the time and the place, a true eyesore. I wasn't jealous, trust me; I was merely suspicious of what was really going on deep inside them, because their diffident and composed mien betrayed the typical demeanor of stage actors. When the beggars approached them, one of the Christians gestured that sinners had no pockets. What hypocrites! I felt no attachment to this place, the land where I was born and raised, and my thoughts shifted to the next train that would take me somewhere else.

It occurred to me that a tiny bullet, the size of a chicken heart, might come in handy. Instead of using it on an enemy, I wanted it to go through my temple and take me away from this place, where my distress had reached its limit. I lived in a tiny corner of society where the members of a bankrupt family had been turned into raw material for manufacturers and prejudice, and where there were very few new ideas. Naturally they were forced, though without knowing it, to use these invisible poisons on me, their oldest son, justified by their belief in familial and moral ethics. When I pulled the trigger, I would die, but would it be considered suicide or homicide?

When I walked past the shoeshine boy, he took one look at shoes that had never enjoyed a shine and knew he needn't bother. The lightning-quick way his expression changed as his eyes moved from my face to my shoes amused me.

I knew there would be nothing for me on the message board, but I walked over anyway.

Yujin: Three trains have gone by, but there's still no sign of you. Waiting is hard on me. Tianmin, on the 28th.

Ah-tian: He knows you know I know. It's all over. Farewell, the 28th.

Zhe: Will do as you wish. Good luck! Mei on the 29th.

I wiped off the old messages and found a piece of chalk to inscribe a few lines of my own:

G: No idea how I ended up at the station; just a sudden urge to leave Yilan with the people here. I'll be in touch; don't worry. M on the 29th.

After I put down the chalk and turned around, I saw that people had been watching me and then reading my message. Embarrassed, I cursed them inwardly: *Mind your own damn business.* I gave them a dirty look, turning the tables by embarrassing them.

The waiting passengers had started to fidget, as if they couldn't wait to leave Yilan and did not care where they went from there. Afraid they might miss their train, they crowded forward to buy tickets, rushed to have the tickets punched, and raced anxiously onto the platform. It didn't seem as if they would miss Yilan, at peace once they stepped onto the platform, as if they were already on their way. *Why don't I leave with them?* The person ahead of me was buying a ticket for Taipei, so I followed suit. I actually did what had merely been a thought when I was writing the message. I couldn't help but be excited by my action as I looked at the ticket in my hand. The emotion kept buoying up, from the moment the light tremor of the train wheels on the tracks thundered against my eardrums to the instant I stepped foot on the train. The wheels began to grind forward, while the sign on the platform with the station name moved backward. I stuck my head out to spit on the sign. It wasn't until I was leaning back in the seat that I began to explain to myself why I'd spat on a sign with the name Yilan on it. I didn't dispute that it was a psychological and symbolic act, but I was puzzled by how my motive had lagged behind my action. It wasn't contrived or coincidental, that was for sure.

At some point someone called out to me, and my vacant gaze fell on the slender legs of the woman across from me. I felt myself banging head-on against the solid wall of reality and, still feeling hazy, engaged in a bit of small talk with the friend from elementary school who had called to me.

"What are you going to do in Taipei?"

"Nothing."

"Nothing?" He raised his voice.

At that point our conversation came to a halt. He sat quietly, a hint of irritation still on his face. I wasn't lying. I wasn't going to Taipei to do anything, and that would be my answer if he asked me a hundred times. My response would always be the same—"Nothing." I was reminded of G when the woman's legs re-entered my field of vision. The farther the train traveled, the more uneasy I became. But my initial excitement returned when I recalled the happy times G and I had shared; I was as happy as the first time I went on a graduation trip.

G had smooth, delicate legs that I found highly attractive. It had taken plenty of planning before I finally managed to take her swimming at Wulaokeng. My interest in taking a dip nearly vanished when I saw her bare legs for the first time, and I was convinced that I wanted to marry her. To be honest, she really did have a rare ability to arouse my desire, which was the major reason I eventually beat out all her other suitors, including the son of a millionaire, a young doctor, and a man whose study abroad made him confident of their future. In her view, I expanded her life experience. Once I took her to Taichung to watch me play in a provincial football match, where she was moved by all the masculinity and strict control, the blood, sacrifice, and combat. I recall the time we beat the team from Kaohsiung. Oblivious to fans who surrounded me and the other players, she ran up, eyes brimming with tears, and grabbed my shoulders with shaking hands. "Please don't play this again," she pleaded. I could see her facial muscles twitching from an internal struggle.

"Don't you see how important I am to the team?"

She nodded. One of the players on my team said, "Hey, you can't have the part of our captain that belongs to our team."

As everyone was roaring, the Kaohsiung team's No. 4 walked by with their No. 9, carrying his shoes and still in uniform. I pushed her away and said, "There's something I have to do." I walked out of the jubilant winner's circle. I called out to No. 4. From the way they were standing there, I could tell that they had come prepared. I was right: he was there to show me up. When I was about three steps away, he rushed up and swung at my face with his cleats. Blocking the blow with my left hand, I landed a right hook and then punched him in the gut, sending him to the ground with a grunt. I heard G scream; she was trying to break free from my teammates Wild Boar and Monk. My hand was bleeding, but she didn't say a word about that and insisted that we go home. My teammates were still talking about the knockout, as Wild Boar feigned my punches. I told G that I had to do it, because the guy had kicked me three times in the crotch during the scrum; I had warned him the first time it happened. G was a woman, after all, and could not understand or accept a lot of things that happened among men.

G had it all over that woman across from me, whose legs lacked some hard-to-describe quality.

Reminiscence brings enjoyment, because it is always pleasant to recall the past. Whether the memory involves glory or degradation, it makes you happy; and the more time that has passed, the better you feel, much like the moment you smell the aroma from a bottle of aged liquor after uncapping it. By the time you're drunk, you've even forgotten what time it is and believe that you are living in the past. That's what happened to me; I forgot I was on a train. The elation I'd felt when I first boarded had given way to recollection. I was looking at mountains outside the window, but that was not what I was seeing. Instead I saw myself carrying a tape recorder to K'yang village with G (I had yet to begin calling her Glakis) and eight indigenous Taiwanese from the village to conduct an interview. Our guide was a village clerk, also from the indigenous tribe, but with a terrific command of Mandarin. Having some doubts about the accuracy of a report from the county to the provincial government, I had decided to go into the mountains to investigate how the K'yang villagers really felt about their land. My superiors did not support my effort, but they humored me, a young reporter who, in their view, needed to burn off some zeal for justice.

We spent two days in the mountains, where everything was new to us. What pleased me most were the names we acquired: she was Glakis and I was Miyasa, which came to us by accident, but nevertheless seemed fitting. I heard the indigenous villagers call out in surprise, "Glakis miyasa" (the girl is so pretty—a comment about her, of course), and we decided to adopt the melodious expression as our names. For some time we had wanted special names, but we could not find any we liked, no matter how we racked our brains. Now they had come to us out of the blue. I did feel somewhat guilty, though, because the names must have enjoyed a primal existence in the mountains for hundreds, maybe thousands, of years, only for us to take them away. She was moved when I told her of my feelings. I shouted spiritedly, "Gla-kis," one syllable at a time, as we were on our way out of the mountains, and she followed my lead by calling out "Mi-ya-sa." The echoes sounded charming and musical, prompting us to repeat our shouts over and over. We even changed pitch and added a simple tune, so amusing the indigenous young men and women who were walking us down the mountain that they joined in. We were so innocent back then, and so touched that tears ran down our faces. After that, we dropped the names our parents gave us when we were together. I called her Glakis (not pronouncing the final "s"), and she called me Miyasa. "I love you, Glakis," I said to her one day, and she replied, "I love you, too, Miyasa." Just like that. We tumbled down a canyon of happiness as if drunk.

I didn't care if the train was too slow or Taipei was too far; I wouldn't have minded if the train had gone in circles. There were a few unhappy passengers who, with apprehension and worry written on their faces, sat slumped in their seats, for there was nothing they could do to change their situation. Some studiously read out the names of every stop, while I could not have cared less. I realized for the first time that not caring could bring me pleasure. A faint tune was playing on a transistor radio. It was one of my favorites, a violin piece by Pablo de Sarasate called "Gypsy Airs." Too bad I caught only the tail end of it. G and I listened to it all the time. G was funny that way; she liked what I liked. I put on sunglasses when I listened to classical music at night indoors, so she went and bought a pair for herself. Sometimes she'd copy me and smoke a cigarette. She was great. I really loved her.

I took her, one step at a time, out of reality and into the realm of art, and a light began to shine in her eyes. I led her to a mirror, where she saw her true self and touched what she wanted to feel; the sensation was something she had never imagined. She told me she was destined to marry me, but I said it could not be predestination. We fought for it, and then she agreed without reservation.

My need for her love was more like greed. I did not dare imagine what it would be like to lose her love or to see her in another man's arms. I knew I would die if that happened. I would, without telling anyone, leave on a dark night for an unfamiliar distant place where I would vanish like a puff of smoke. *Just like that*, I said to myself, as I saw bluish smoke rise in a distant field and merge with the clouds. Looking down, I checked my body, especially the uncovered parts, letting my gaze roam over them, even touching them. It was impossible to imagine the process that would turn this solid physicality into drifting smoke. My heart stirred when I scrutinized my skin and pressed down hard with my hands, as if my body were about to separate from my consciousness. The sensation was so strong that I could have mistaken it as an effect of masturbation. But no, absolutely not, though the feelings were similar; it was like two types of perfume that you cannot tell apart.

But then I realized that I would very much want G to come see me before I died. She was easily frightened, so I mustn't scare her. My soul would adjust the position of my body after it departed. I would choose to lie down at a spot with rose bushes, of course. As my soul left my body, it would not like the way I was lying—too stiff, with my face up and a bit frightening. I should be lying with my right hand pillowing my head and my left hand falling naturally to the side. My legs should bend a bit, not stick out straight; I should look like I'm asleep. Oh, and my hair had to be smoothed down. My eyes would be closed, the lashes sealed together with tears, while my facial muscles must be slack and my head bent down slightly. My soul would back away for another look and be pleased with what it saw. The gentle sun would shine down through the leaves and branches of the rose bushes, like petals sprinkled over my body. It would dry the tears, my soul would say, as it moved a branch to block the sunlight. Inspired by the dazzling rays, it would pick roses to spread their petals atop my corpse. If my head seemed too low, it would walk over to adjust the position. *That's it*, it would say. *Don't move. Oh! I don't think you'll ever move again.* The soul would place a tender kiss on my face. *Wait here. G will come see you soon. I will hide behind a tree to watch her cry sadly over you. I will tell you she still loves you very much. She will cry over your death.*

"Ticket, please." Someone shook my shoulder. I looked up

with a blank stare, sending two teardrops sliding down my face. "Sorry. Could I see your ticket, please?" the startled conductor said politely.

I knew he was apologetic over my tears and felt sorry for what he imagined was my sad past. I thrust my ticket at him unceremoniously; I loathed misunderstandings caused by foolish people's overconfidence, which happened all the time. He was being nice, but I found it hard to overlook the degree of his stupidity and its resulting consequence. Soon, however, my agitation died down and was shoved aside by other, more insistent thoughts. The woman was sitting with her legs spread. G would never demean herself that way.

At the time, G was giving me so much love that when I thought it over carefully, I knew I was the luckiest man alive. Yet I tensed at the fear that I might disappoint her, and I found the burden of my responsibility nearly impossible to bear. I knew, from what she had given me, that it would not be enough for me to be an ordinary, meek husband. At the same time, however, her urgent love for me had a hint of preconception that was annoying and hard to accept, owing to that fear, which she would, in turn, mistake for a rejection of her love; that would pain her so much that she would hurt me intentionally. When a woman's love is mixed up with her preconceptions, the man who loves her and whom she loves will be like a famished dog staring at a chunk of electrified beef, afraid to move forward yet reluctant to back off, torn helplessly by the dilemma. G was no exception, and I had to give up my freedom and struggle to survive the suffocation. I was frightened by her love, but could not live without it. It would have been perfect if her love had not made me anxious with its inconsistency. But then it wouldn't have been human, because human beings are full of contradictions, especially where love is involved. I managed to assuage my doubts.

Large raindrops fell on my cheek, stinging a bit, as if someone were flinging mud at me. It continued to rain even when the sun came out again. Half a rainbow hung in the sky, the type that fishermen back home called "a tailless monkey," the sign of a looming typhoon. Indeed, the radio said that Betty would hit land the next day. Many of the passengers in window seats stuck their heads out to look at the rainbow, all with the same expression on their faces, acting in unison; the only thing they cared about was the dramatic change predicted in the next day's weather. That was not surprising, since they had all had disastrous experiences, and the radio made the typhoon sound like a serious threat. Her voice shaking, the woman announced that the wind speed was going to reach a hundred meters per second. I was sure the other passengers heard that.

Every time we stopped at a station, I could tell that the wind was picking up, but that did not mean the force would necessarily be stronger as we headed north. Every person on the train knew that the typhoon was drawing ever closer to their hometown. Dry brown pinecones were the first to fall, followed by green ones that jumped up and down on the grass atop the red soil, as if dancing to welcome the typhoon's arrival. The gale swept them over to a windless hollow, where they lay motionless, as if displaced. They were like children who laugh one moment and cry the next when they can't find their way home. It made me happy to think about them, happy but sorry.

Once I'd picked up a few to play with. Inanimate objects can come alive when we find similarities between them and us. G, I was in a great mood when I went to mail you a letter. It was being loved by you that allowed me to study pinecones and engage in such an intricate thought process. The world in my eyes must have had a rosy glow, just like the one you saw.

It was on the eve of another typhoon two years before when I felt the warmth of pinecones in my hand. Since then we have loved each other intensely. The pine trees beyond the train window quaked in the wind; at least I thought they did, because they had looked so uncomfortable that time I'd picked up their cones.

A driving rainsquall beat down on us. I was the only passenger who shut his window, which I discovered after I'd done it, but that had nothing to do with the unhappy looks I got from the other passengers. The air in the car was stifling, though to me it was more because of the passengers' moods, which seemed to be affected by every molecule of air going in and out of their lungs. The thought made me want to open the window, and then the rain stopped, giving me the excuse I needed. The sky cleared, but only briefly, because dusk had taken hold by then, much like the sudden downpour earlier. From behind the layers of clouds came sunlight, which lost its oppressive power when it was reflected on the aluminum window frames; I no longer felt as if a sword were pressing down on my forehead.

Someone was selling the evening newspaper from Taipei, which had been brought to our train when it met the one going from Taipei to Su-ao. From the way the vendor hawked his wares, I could tell that he was an old hand—he had a feverish voice that enticed people to buy from him. The pages of the paper, carrying news about the typhoon, were spread across men's legs. The passengers wore their moods on their faces, though some kind of order still prevailed amid the chaos. With their heads buried in their newspapers, they reminded me of soldiers heading into battle.

Up till that moment, I had not felt lonely in my own world, which could have been painful but was actually gratifying. I was different, I told myself, and that was why others suffered over their monotonous lives. The young man next to me handed me his paper and confidently waited to be rewarded with my gratitude. Once again I was irritated by the overconfidence of foolish people and the resultant misunderstanding. I refused to even look at him; instead, I stuck my head out into the rain so the refreshing experience could confirm my existence. I could only speculate on what was going on in his head, and could not have cared less about his feelings. Granted, I did not own a house and had nothing to my name but my life, so a powerful typhoon posed no threat to me. As for my life, the pain I'd endured told me that I was resilient. More importantly, there is no need to fear the inevitability of death once you recognize the essence of life. I hoped this view would not mislead people into thinking I was stressing the merits of poverty. I had never felt poor, at least not until the night G came running to see me and said amid happy tears, "Miyasa, my family has finally agreed to let us marry." No one but I could have understood her irrepressible joy at that moment, and G imagined that I would react the same way. So she was dumbfounded by my unusual calm. Her happy news had brought forth real-life issues we had never considered. Everyone who met her was convinced that she was a wonderful girl who would lead a good life, but I wondered if she could change enough to live compatibly with me. If not, my conscience would suffer even if she didn't. I gave her a solemn description of my feelings: "I'm sorry, dear Glakis. I should be even happier than you are. But at this moment, I don't have time to be happy, because suddenly

I feel that I'm the most impoverished man on earth. It isn't just a feeling, actually, it's the truth. I didn't know it before and have always considered myself a rich man. I know this inner turmoil is caused by the realization that I will be responsible for you from now on. I'm so afraid of disappointing you or causing you pain. I love you too much."

She seemed heavy when I held her in my arms, yet the weight came not from her, but from a breathless reality. I thought I would die of suffocation.

"How can I prove to you that you've changed me? I'm a completely different person. Please believe me, Miyasa," she said. Suddenly she felt so light in my arms that she might as well have been weightless. I wished with all my heart that she were heavy enough to crush me; I would not have complained. We celebrated our victory with endless sweet kisses.

***

The force of the typhoon was no threat. I needed to revise my motivation for boarding the train: I wasn't leaving with these people; the train was taking me somewhere else. The revision was made necessary by the young man, who tried to put as much distance between us as possible.

An eye-catching hotel sign in a large town flashed past the window. I fixed my gaze on it until the train had moved on too far for me to see. It was not the hotel where G and I had spent our first night together, of course. That was impossible—we had never considered coming to this place.

We were at a hotel entrance, having reached the point at which we could no longer hide our desire as we roamed the streets of an unknown city. I had to whisper when I noticed how she looked, "At least neither of us thinks this is wrong. But the way you look now will convince the hotel staff that we're doing something illicit. Take a deep breath and think of something funny so you'll have a smile on your face."

"That comment alone is enough to make me laugh," she said with a smile.

I recall that it was Room 36, with two windows looking out onto the streets and a factory smokestack. G saw the number and said it was the same as the one on my jersey. She looked tense, actually, seeming to feel the need to be alert to our new surroundings. Based on previous experience, I knew that the way to make her relax was to tell her a story. She once said that she had never met anyone who was better at storytelling than I. I could recall every detail of the story, a fairy tale.

Once upon a time there was an artist who found a fine slab of marble and wanted to carve a bust of the perfect woman. The image of that woman emerged after a prolonged period, during which the artist's determination was pitted against the stone's stubborn nature. He was overcome by her beauty and nearly driven mad by his infatuation with the lifeless stone sculpture. The gods, touched by his consummate love, poured life into the sculpture in the spring, when even nameless wild flowers remembered to bloom, and they were married.

G was unhappy that I hadn't told her the story earlier. Circumstances dictate the kind of story to tell, I said; it was a matter of ambience. She added that it was very much the story of our life together; I was the artist, and she was the marble sculpture given life after it was completed. I was glad to hear that.

"I must go look for a job in Taipei to support us after we get married," I told her a couple of days later.

"Do you really want to do that?" She knew I'd never liked Taipei, for a variety of reasons. "Like you, I can't stand to live there."

"For our life together, we can't worry about whether we want to or not. You must be pragmatic now," I said, straining against my true feelings.

"That's terrible." She blanched. Struggling to stay calm, she repeated the fairy tale I'd told her in Room 36. But her ending went like this: The god was late in giving the sculpture life, so by the time she was alive, the lovelorn artist had already died of longing at her feet. With her arms around the artist, she pleaded with the god to take back her life.

"You've changed me. Now you're abandoning me and running away after taking me to this beautiful place." We could not find any middle ground, so she repeated what I'd said to her. The solid sensation of the self was gone. How would I pull myself together? I felt utterly ashamed in front of her.

***

The train reached its destination, Taipei. I hadn't made the trip for the purpose of getting there; I had merely wanted to leave Yilan and go somewhere else, a place that obviously remained elusive. I didn't know why, but I felt something like dire emptiness and despair when I stepped down onto the platform. I tried to gauge the seriousness of having that kind of emotional reaction. The other place I longed to go very likely did not exist in any time or space. I cursed myself. I'd been tricked. Yes. I'd been duped by the foolish overconfidence that courses in the blood of the human race. The supposition that one can actually cast off psychological shackles was an irresistible temptation to someone suffering from angst and ennui.

Everyone but me stepped spryly onto the platform as if they were coming home. Besieged by sorrow, I didn't feel like going anywhere but home, back to G. I experienced the distress of a lost child calling out for his mother. Glakis. You would be pleased if you knew how I missed you. It seemed as if I had never been so far from home, and I felt disoriented.

Taipei station was crowded, as always. Swarms of people were waiting at the telecommunication counter to make long-distance calls; the interminable wait almost killed me. Holding the handset, I felt my hand go numb just before the call went through, as if I had to squeeze it hard to calm down. I could see that the blood had drained from my tensed arm.

Finally an emotional but tiny voice came to me from a faraway place, like a miracle. "I've been looking all over for you, Miyasa. How could you take off for Taipei without telling me?"

I could see her in my mind's eye, crying emotionally while her co-workers stopped in mid-conversation to look at her, some shaking their heads, others wondering why she'd fallen for a man who brought her nothing but grief. Seized by an irrepressible rage, I could not talk for a moment, causing her to call out anxiously, "Say something, Miyasa. I want to hear your voice, Miyasa. Hello? Hello? Anyone at the telecom office?" I heard the sound of her tapping the hook switch on the phone. "Hello? You at the telecomm office."

It pained me that she was so worried, so I broke the silence. "Glakis!" Just calling out her name was enough to sap my strength. I felt like a sheet of paper being slowly torn apart.

"What happened? Are you all right?"

"I'm fine, Glakis. I just want to be back with you."

"Then hurry back, Miyasa. There's one last train left."

"It leaves in an hour. I'll take it."

"I'll be waiting for you at the station." She sounded elated.

"Yes, do. I'll be looking for you." I couldn't wait to see her. Even one second without her felt like an eternity at that moment.

"I'll be there."

"Make sure you are," I stressed, knowing that it was unnecessary. She would be there. It was disrespectful to remind her like that, and I was ashamed.

"I will be there." She changed her tone and asked, "How's the wind in Taipei?"

"It's getting stronger."

"The typhoon will make landfall at Yilan at three tomorrow morning. The weather bureau has issued its final warning." She sounded worried.

"We'll be together by then." I tried to put her mind at ease.

"Be careful on your way back. The wind is getting stronger by the minute. Are you all right?"

"I'm fine."

"Hurry back, please."

"My heart is already on its way."

"I'll be waiting for you at the station."

"Make sure to be there." I had done it again. I felt pangs of shame from the unintentional reminder.

"You're horrible. I'll have to punish you when you get back. I'll die if you run off without a word again." It sounded like a pout.

"I left a message for you at the Yilan train station."

"What did you write?"

"Let's not waste time on that."

"I'm going to go read it." She was suddenly reminded of something. "Do you have money?"

"I think I still have some left." Actually, I wasn't sure.

A chime sounded to tell us our time was up.

"That's enough, then. I'll be waiting for you at the station," G said.

"Make sure you're there." I didn't care about pangs in my heart now, so long as I could hold on to the hope. I made excessive demands on her.

My indecision had lessened, but my overall mood of apprehension had not improved. I didn't think I could wait quietly until the next train left in an hour, but I had no idea what I could do to fill the time. Sit in the station like an idiot? That would amount to unbearable boredom, like counting every second till I reached three thousand and six hundred.

My only consolation was that the last train would take me home and to G, who was waiting for me there. My confidence had vanished since the last time I tasted success, but now I was content that I could restore my self-assurance with that promise from her over the phone. She had said that she would wait for me, and I felt sure of that. *She'll be there, she will,* I repeated tirelessly to myself.

It was getting dark. The Taipei streetlights accomplished their mission of bridging day and night. When the traffic lights were red, they seemed to be close together, while when the lights turned green, they seemed to crawl, moving in laborious unison. Crowds of pedestrians converged at intersections, then quickly dispersed, over and over. They moved in such even, uniform, mechanical intervals that I was reminded of the conveyor belt at a factory I once visited. There was a typhoon coming, but Taipei looked no different from any other day, as if the residents were unaware of it. Their composure made me aware of the city's animosity toward me, like they were showing off their sense of superiority—we're in our own houses now, and we'll worry about it if and when it happens. My self-assurance began to crack. If I were to find a job here, would I be able to survive in this environment? I came to this conclusion: *I'll tell G the moment I get off the train tonight that I hate Taipei and don't want to work here. We won't even say the city's name. It's such an unevenly developed place that our emotional equilibrium would suffer once we were here. Neither of us wants to be a Taipei resident.* I was sure she'd be happy to hear me say that. She would be waiting for me at the station, and I would see her happy face again.

Another gust of wind brought bean-size drops of rain. Under the glare of the streetlights and the automobiles' headlights, the road surface looked like it was shrouded in a layer of low-lying fog. The yellow "Vacant" lights atop taxicabs drifted in the dark, dank air like fireflies. If I'd had the money, I would have called out "Taxi" and let it take me all the way to Yilan. That would be so gratifying. I wished I could see G now. *No, I agreed to meet her at the train station, and she'll make sure to be there,* I said silently, probably to make myself feel better about not having enough money.

I stayed close to the station, since I had told her I'd take the last train back. Afraid of missing my train, I walked a few steps and quickly turned back. I lined up behind the few people at the ticket window; there was no need to hurry, but it helped to kill time. When it was my turn, I took out twelve NT, all the money I had. The ticket seller asked impatiently where I wanted to go. I said Yilan.

"Nineteen NT for Yilan."

"How far can I go with twelve NT?" I tensed up.

"Fulong."

"I'll go to Fulong, then."

Without even looking up, he tossed me the ticket after some quick hand movements and the sound of metal on metal. Holding a ticket that would take me only halfway, I felt an intense internal struggle. I have to return to Yilan; G will be there to meet me. I have to find a way, no matter what; I'll pay the difference when I get to Yilan station. She'll be there.

I thought about looking for someone I knew to borrow ten NT. It wouldn't be hard to run into an acquaintance at the station, not hard at all. My eyes swept through the crowd, and within a minute I had spotted three people. One of them, a young county clerk, was in a crowd watching TV; the second one, reading the evening paper below the TV, was an elementary school teacher; and the third, the owner of the Jide Fabric Shop, was spread out in his chair, a pile of flesh, his hands folded atop his potbelly, his crossed feet shaking nervously. I casually walked up to him. He addressed me as a reporter when he saw me. I told him I'd quit my job. He asked what I was doing now, and I said I was unemployed. With a laugh he patted me on the shoulder, implying that I was trying to be secretive. With that kind of opening, I knew I'd blown it. He would pat my shoulder again and laugh even louder if I asked to borrow ten NT. If I tried to explain, a rumor might start about an unemployed reporter making a living by borrowing ten NT here and twenty NT there at the Taipei train station. I had heard such gossip about others in the past, and I couldn't have something like that said about me. So the idea of borrowing from him flashed through my mind and then vanished. A sense of awakening stopped me from walking up to the elementary school teacher and drove the idea of borrowing money out of my mind. I would do what I had decided to do earlier: pay the difference when I got to Yilan. G would be there waiting for me.

A hint of self-reproach took hold. I nearly died of embarrassment as I tried to suppress the image of me acting like a clown and sacrificing my dignity. I went to sit in an empty seat where people who knew me wouldn't see me, and where I could silently while away the seemingly interminable waiting time. I couldn't stop thinking that if I ever lost my resolve, I would turn into one of those sad sacks I'd always despised, maybe even a different person altogether. The new me would share the same body, arguing incessantly over the same things from different perspectives, until they both disappeared once my body decomposed. That thought led me back to the source of my suffering. I could only hear hurried and labored breathing amid noise that sounded as if it were struggling to emerge from a heavy darkness. Another friend walked up to sit by me, but my desire to talk was long gone. At one point he said, "It's about time; let's go over to the platform." I didn't move until he set foot on the platform. A ray of happiness over my homecoming lit up the darkness in my heart, but it quickly died out, owing to my eagerness. A sudden downpour left no dry spot on the platform and sent the waiting passengers scurrying to the overhead walkway or onto the staircase.

A primitive competition started the moment the train entered the station. Most of the young men were able to grab seats, owing to some superior quality they possessed, as were a few old men and women. I put my hand down on the seat beside me. A bespectacled middle-aged man came up with an obsequious smile and asked me if the seat was taken. I ignored him because he had a striking resemblance to my section chief. He stood there looking hopeful. Then a fashionably dressed young woman came through the door and walked down the aisle searching for an empty seat. I gave it to her, because I preferred having her next to me. G was still on my mind, and no one could take her place. I wanted the woman next to me, but not because I was being unfaithful. Why was it, then? Just natural, I guessed. I ignored her after sizing her up coolly, though I could tell she would have liked to start up a conversation.

My window seemed to be the only one open in a car that would be sealed up if I closed it. But the rain outside was coming down so hard I had to give in and shut it, albeit reluctantly. Inside, the air turned stiflingly hot, even with the overhead fans straining to stir the mucky air suffused with bloated molecules. I was irritable and knew that I could blow up at the slightest provocation, because I felt like a total screw-up. Keeping my eyes on the window, I was ready to open it the moment the rain died down, but the heavy drops continued to slam against the windowpane, sending a torrential gush down the surface. Lightning flashed occasionally in the distance. The image of my upper body was reflected in the window, and a pair of tortured eyes stared back at me, a startlingly alien expression. The gauntness of my face was highlighted all out of proportion by my profile, and I found the cold, harsh gaze disturbing.

Make sure you do it. Make sure. It means not changing a thing and, on my part, making sure to return. I have to go back home. Filled with worry, I kept reminding myself; I felt utterly miserable as I fingered the halfway ticket in my hand. I hadn't wanted to go home this badly since I was old enough to understand what went on in life. I was eager to go back, but not for the clouds in the sky or the famous rain; home for me was wherever G was. It might be a selfish thought, but the less I suffered, the less sorrow she'd feel. I didn't want her to shed sad tears because of me; it was painful to imagine those tears, let alone see them. I hoped there were strong enough feelings between us for her to sense their existence, though I didn't really have to worry about that, for that had brought us together. I just didn't want her to be sad because of me, and most of all, I didn't want her to cry when I failed to show up at the station later that evening. The scene was not hard to imagine:

The train finally reaches Yilan. G is standing by the gate along with the other people who have come to meet passengers. She is on tiptoes, craning her neck, her bright, anxious eyes searching for me among the travelers rushing off the cars. Her face tightens with each passing second. The passengers race through the gate, and everyone around her leaves with whomever they came to meet. Only her pale face remains at the gate. The train starts up again, and the platform becomes deathly quiet when the last traveler hands his ticket to the collector at the gate. Rain is pouring down in the gale-force winds. Her long black hair is a tangled mess across her face, disheveled like her scattered thoughts. Feeling a sudden light-headedness, she crouches with her hands over her face. Amid the howling rain and wind, she seems to hear my promise: "Glakis, I'll be coming home on the last train, so make sure to come and meet me at the station." She drops her hands to look at the platform, which is more desolate than ever. The gate bars and metal posts all seem twisted in her eyes. She dries her tears, but soon everything in her field of vision turns eerie, devoid of its original features. Reality is too cruel for her to take in. Cradling my brown jacket and our raincoats, she walks out, oblivious to the rain and wind coming at her. Tears ooze from the place where she hurts most, making it impossible to tell them from the rain. "Glakis! Glakis!" Of course she can't hear me. "It's too late, Glakis, and with this storm, you shouldn't be going that way. Go home, go home now." Of course she can't hear me. She is already walking down the road by the river, where we used to catch fireflies. One time we caught a few dozen of them and took them back to my room, where we let them flit in our happiness after we closed the door and turned off the lights. She really is going that way. "Please go home, Glakis. Please. Don't go there, please." I was startled awake when I heard myself shout in my reverie. Naturally, I turned to check the woman next to me; she was looking at me with surprise in her eyes. "Did you have a bad dream?" she asked. I closed my eyes and shook my head, meaning it was not a dream. I had the feeling that something terrible was about to happen.

    I needed a brief moment, Glakis, for some peace and quiet. My agitation and suffering were all because of you. Leaning my head against the window, I stretched my legs out to loosen up. At some point I tensed up again, shifting my body this way and that, unable to find a comfortable position. I was driven to distraction by sitting in the train and could barely keep from jumping off to run to her. The train wasn't moving fast enough for me. Something had to happen, either to lighten my mood or to make the situation worse. I would suffer a nervous breakdown if everything stayed the same and I was forever tormented and waiting anxiously. But no one could do anything about it. It seemed that the whole situation had been prearranged, with the process and outcome all planned out. I could feel as edgy as I wanted, but that would not help one bit, I told myself. I abruptly felt calm returning when the thought flashed through my jumbled mind. I noticed, for the first time since I had gotten on, that the train was slowly leaving a station. The rain had stopped briefly, but the wind was still blowing hard. I opened the window and stuck my head out to take in some fresh air in the darkness. I was halfway out the window when someone tugged at me. I retreated inside as the woman said, "You were talking to yourself, and what I thought you were about to do just now terrified me. I hope it was just my imagination." She reached over and shut the window. The ticket collector walked up before I could respond, and asked for my ticket. I gave him a blank look; he had obviously sensed that I was in trouble. A smirk appeared on his face for no discernible reason as he repeated his demand. *I hope we haven't reached Fulong yet*, I said to myself as I looked out the window to see where we were. He took my ticket and held it. "We just passed Fulong. You can get off at Dali without paying the difference." He was pleased with himself. Clearly he thought I wanted to a free ride and wouldn't be happy until he had a chance to embarrass me.

"I'm going to Yilan." I was incensed over his intention to humiliate me.

"Then you'll have to pay the difference," he said in a leisurely manner that personified his superiority.

"I'll do that when I get to Yilan. Someone is waiting for me there."

"I'm sorry, sir," he said mockingly. "I'd like to help you, but we have to follow the rules, which for me are an order. I can't help you. What if every passenger asked to do the same thing? You look like a smart guy, but I can't make an exception for you." His smiling face was the very object I'd always wanted to smash.

I felt dizzy, but he wouldn't relent.

"We'll reach Dali after this tunnel. Be prepared to get off there or borrow money from someone," he continued smugly.

I had thought I'd be able to appeal to his compassion, but I would rather die than look submissive to someone like him.

He had raised his voice and told me to borrow money. I was so mortified I couldn't look at the people around me. I'd die of shame if someone I knew were watching me at that moment. My rage had gathered and solidified in my right fist. I glared at him; he tried to provoke me with another smirk. Fury rose up inside to the point that I thought I'd blow up; I relaxed my fist and fought back tears. No, not in front of someone like him. I was able to uncurl my fist only by clenching my teeth; and just before making a serious mistake, I thought about how much worse off I'd be if I were to hit him. I hurried toward the door after the train came out of the tunnel and jumped off when it had barely entered the station, getting drenched in the process.

We were nearly at the entrance to the Lanyang Plain when the train came out of the southbound tunnel. To my left was the Pacific Ocean, where a small country road stretched toward Yilan. These places were familiar to me. I could have found shelter in the train station or at a fisherman's house, if not for my singular, burning desire to get home. Yilan was thirty kilometers away, but I refused to give up my most uncompromising wish to go home, to go back to G.

It was so black I couldn't see a thing, but intuition and experience made my current situation clear. The typhoon had landed; it was not unusual that it had arrived a few hours off the time predicted by the weather bureau. The ocean was roiling. From a few hundred meters away, the waves, mixed with torrential rain and sand from the beach, and sometimes with twigs and leaves, roared at me again and again. At first they stung my exposed skin, but soon I was too numb to feel anything. I had to turn my face to the side in order to breathe. The wind came from the left, so I turned sideways and bent forward as I strained against it. Trying to keep as low a profile as possible, I took one slow step at a time, each the price my will had to pay to get through all my tribulations. Sometimes the wind was so strong I had to squat down and wait before starting off again. Soon my eyes began to function better in the oppressive darkness of the rain and wind; I could just about make out a murky light when the rain beat down on the road surface a meter or two ahead of me. It was even clearer when I crouched down. A sensation somewhere between seeing and feeling was the reason, and also the secret, why I wouldn't veer off the road. My only hope was to keep heading south, relying on this road and the barely detectable murky light.

After covering a considerable distance, I could no longer feel the existence of other parts of my body, only my clear head, as if I were dragging a heavy object I'd stumbled upon in the dark. What lay before me was time and my life, all tied up with my quickly fading willpower. I wasn't sure how far I had come, but I knew I was heading south and would eventually reach G. I jogged when I could; once my left foot got stuck in a hole on the road and I fell. My cheek scraped against the road; it burned painfully. I could have gotten up and continued to run, but I didn't. Instead I lay there to assess my situation. That made me laugh. The storm had picked up. I might have been only ten or twenty meters away from the ocean, for seawater was splashing on me, making my cheek burn even more. Maybe it would feel better if I got up and walked. But I'd barely taken a few steps before a gust of wind knocked me over. I kept walking. I was sure I was heading south, sure I hadn't veered off the road, and sure that I was one step closer to G. But then again, I had a feeling that I was stumbling into more darkness and moving away from G, and that I would be forever lost in time with no tomorrow. The train station and G's pale, despairing face reminded me that action was of the utmost importance at that moment; I would be able to save myself only through action and for action's sake. My life was linked to my willpower now, and I realized what G meant to me.

The storm intensified, and the darkness deepened with my every step. It felt like the end of the world. Amid the din from the shrill and bleak howls coming from everything around me, I heard someone shout at the top of his lungs, "Glakis!" It sounded like me, but I couldn't be sure.

1966

The Face in the Mirror

In today's society, it was mortifying for a forty-year-old dirt-poor man like Aben to look at himself in a mirror.

But on this morning, the day the construction of the new Fishermen's Association headquarters was completed, the head of his company's general affairs section had hurriedly arranged for the congratulatory gift of a large, three-by-four-foot mirror; the red ink of the inscriptions on each side was still wet. It was Aben's job to deliver it to the opening ceremony. Seated on the three wheeler, he held on to the mirror as the general affairs section head and several of his curious office mates came out to watch him depart. Curious? Maybe not. Looking at the mirror? To a degree, maybe. They probably weren't sure why they were out there. So best to write it off as curiosity.

"Be careful with that mirror, Aben!" The personnel chief's shout and his office mates' laughter fell in behind him.

"I know … don't worry!" Aben turned to return the shout, but inside he was seething. "Damn. That's crap! I'm not some three-year-old."

With the mirror facing him, he saw himself reflected in it from head to toe, which in turn gave him the feeling that there were two of him on the three wheeler, though the fellow up front was getting paid for only one. But before he could start thinking about anything else, he reminded himself of the unsettling fact that he was riding on a three wheeler. As a poor man with low self-esteem, he felt self-conscious about the ride, which was a luxury for him. So he kept an apprehensive eye out for anyone he might know.

They hit a bump in the road, causing the mirror to rock back and forth. Aben suddenly had no time for thoughts of inferiority. He clutched the frame with both hands and focused on holding it steady. He saw a strange Aben sitting in front of him. He knew he was looking at himself, but the longer he looked, the more he wondered—*Is that really what I'm like? Yeah, that's you, all right. A dud.* He mocked his own image. He recognized the features, but the overall effect was weird. He was becoming a stranger to himself, to the point that the image was unrecognizable, and that feeling was a psychological mystery he was incapable of putting into words, as if he were floating in a void. He had to struggle to stabilize himself. He shut his eyes and began to think hard. And still that image was staring back at the blank look on his face—a man. Now he was good and truly scared. Of what? He didn't know. But whatever it was, he kept his eyes shut. That didn't work. He could still see the man in the mirror. Time to change positions. Before too long he was back floating in the void, and as far as the reflection that wouldn't go away was concerned, he was already regretting having doubts about his image as he started out. Though he wasn't aware of it, the act of regret had seriously diminished his fear of his own reflection. The regret he felt over his image was that of a helpless weakling, feeling repentant as he faced an omnipotent god. He tried not to have any more doubts about his reflection, actually forced himself to believe in it. *Everybody needs examine his appearance every once in a while,* he said to himself. *If you don't look in a mirror frequently, you stand the chance of being shocked by your own image. I haven't looked at myself in a mirror for I don't know how long.* He knew it was a mistake, but instead of going to a barbershop, he waited until an itinerant barber, one without a mirror, could come by the house to cut his hair, so he could save three yuan each time. He thought back: *Oh, no! It's so long. I've saved a lot of three yuans! How long has it been since I looked in a mirror?*

When he was a boy, he used to sneak his older sister's hand mirror out to the threshing floor to play with in the sunlight. The last time he did that, he recalled, he had a great time.

It was the day before the Dragon Boat Festival. Under the punishing rays of the sun, Grandma had lined up all his father's and uncles' kids, from youngest to eldest, to shave their heads in the shade of a thorny bamboo grove by the river. All against the wishes of the kids themselves. She scared them by saying that ghosts would come and take their hair to tie up *zongzi*. The word "ghosts" made them grit their teeth and submit to the ordeal, begging Grandma to be careful with the razor. But her scare tactics had little effect on young Aben. He'd heard it all before. He hated having his head shaved, thought it was an act of cruelty, and nothing, not trickery and not intimidation, could change his attitude. His sister's mirror in hand, he ran out into the sunlight and hid in some peanut vines across the river, where he aimed the mirror at Axian's face. With the blinding light in his eyes, Axian tilted his head up just as Grandma was scraping it with her razor, resulting in a gash that sent blood trickling down over his face and horrified Grandma. She frantically bent down, scooped up a handful of hair, soaked it in soapy water, and pressed it against the bleeding wound, the soapy mix dragging shrieks of pain from him. Eight more heads awaited shaving, all belonging to children who had dreaded the event to begin with, and who had now lost all confidence in Grandma's barbering skills. The adults in the family managed with some difficulty and the destruction of countless peanut shoots to get their hands on Aben. They tied him with ropes and strung him up so his feet couldn't touch the ground.

All his misdeeds to this point—the partial destruction of a peanut crop and his uncle's ripped pants, which had nearly cost him his testicles on the horns of the family bull during the walk home from a neighbor's house where Aben had taken the bull for a bullfight—came to a head that day. He wasn't given a single zongzi to eat on the holiday. He must have been eight that year, he thought, as he sat on the three wheeler. He took another look at the mirror and was greeted by a more agreeable face.

Then there was another incident, the first of the two times he'd looked at himself in a mirror. Aben's father had asked someone to borrow a dark blue lined silk jacket from the village head, a Mr. Zheng from Dingcuo. Aben's heart raced as he tried it on in front of the mirror on Grandma's vanity, the smell of mothballs filling his nostrils. He was going to enter the bridal chamber with a woman that night. Aju, how was she different from any other woman? He had never laid eyes on her, but she was definitely a woman. He was nineteen, and Grandma had often told him how happy she'd be to see him married before she died. "In the eyes of society, you aren't a man until you're married," she said. "The villager Tianfu has a nice, well-behaved daughter who would be ideal if they think we're good enough for them. Auntie Fanpo came by today to seek our views. I never thought anybody would be interested in a buffalo like you." Grandma was so emotional, she actually cried.

Aben had often heard older boys talk about women, so he had been itching for action. It didn't matter who Aju was, since this is how village people got married. It was how Father had married Mother and how Grandma had married Grandpa. Grandma was always going on about marriage being settled by a person's fate. Aben could still conjure up what he looked like in Grandma's mirror at the age of nineteen, his face turning red from surprise and happiness. In the bridal chamber that night, his bride kept her head low, weighed down by the head gear and ornaments, as she sat on the edge of the eight-footed bed with her legs hanging down, as if in waiting. Aben didn't know what to do, either. He stood there and looked at her, a robust young woman with big hips, the type made to have babies. The thought of having children made him a little uncomfortable. His throat itched, and he wanted to say something to break the ice over the awkwardness, but when he opened his mouth, all he could manage was a bashful cough. His bride looked up at him and let her eyes sweep past his clothes. "I borrowed that jacket from Village Head Zheng," he rushed to explain, to his surprise, but stopped there. He wished he hadn't said it, and now he was really nervous. As if someone were pushing him from behind, he pressed his bride down on the bed, still fully clothed. And exactly nine months later, Grandma was holding a roly-poly baby boy in her arms.

Back on the three wheeler, Aben saw the man in the mirror smile. The smiling face resembled the one in Grandma's vanity mirror on his wedding day, when he was nineteen. It was much thinner now, the forehead replete with wrinkles that had suddenly appeared over the past few years. The healthy glow was a thing of the past. He took careful stock of his features, one at a time, and noticed several black flyspecks on the mirror surface. As he let go of the frame, his face twitched, and he recalled another instance—a summer day four years earlier—in front of a mirror.

Aben was very sick and did not know how long he'd been like that. When he came to after being unconscious for days, his head seemed filled with cobwebs, and yet he was so alert it was almost scary. He looked down at his arms, which were as thin and dry as kindling, and reached up to rub his face. What he wanted more than anything at that moment was a mirror, so he could see just how gaunt he'd gotten. He rolled over with great difficulty, which so exhausted him it was all he could manage. His two youngest children were lying between him and the drawer that held the mirror. *Where are the other five? What time is it? And Aju, where did she go?* His two undernourished kids were asleep, not a care in the world, probably dreaming about sitting down at a groaning dinner table; it was heartbreaking to see them. He propped himself up on shaky arms and, taking care not to squash them, managed to get his hands on Aju's mirror. He took a hard look at himself: he was skin and bones, with sunken eyes and jutting cheekbones. He didn't recognize himself at first, but knew it had to be him. This was something he'd never expected, and his first thoughts were of dying. That scared him. He felt dizzy, he couldn't move his arms or legs, and he fell back weakly. *I should have died, I really should have, instead of making them suffer ...*

He felt a bit better after a while, a little more clearheaded and slightly stronger, so he slid off the bed and crawled into the kitchen. The moment he laid his hand on the cleaver, his strength left him, and he saw that the cleaver was now lying on the floor beside him. He lacked the strength to pick it up, and was wracked by pitiful sobs. Aju, who had been out doing people's laundry, walked in, saw what had happened, and ran up to take Aben in her arms. Through her tears, she said: "What a fool you are. What did you think you were doing? A few days ago I saw a fortune-teller who told me that thirty-nine is a bad year for you, but things will get better when you get past it. Thirty-nine is a terrible beast. Don't be a fool. Everything is decided by fate, and there's nothing we can do about it. You can't die, Aben …" She sobbed and could not go on. Then, through her tears, she said, "A reporter came to the house a few days ago and wrote us up in the paper. People have been sending us money ever since, and things we can use, lots of them. I tell you, it's all decided by fate! It's true. Heaven has eyes, so we will be able to go on. Not only that, but a company sent word that there is a job waiting for you when you get better."

"Aben, everything is decided by fate." To Aben, it felt like Aju was there talking to him. His recollections brought tears to his eyes. The fellow pedaling up front spotted the Fishermen's Association headquarters up ahead and heard the faint sound of firecrackers going off. He pedaled harder.

They were almost there. Strings of firecrackers at the entrance were popping. A crowd had gathered around the celebratory floral wreaths, and musicians had begun playing for the ceremony, but Aben's thoughts were elsewhere: he was gazing blankly at the man in the mirror. When they reached the entrance, the driver slammed on the brakes, sending Aben and the mirror forward. The back of the mirror bumped into the driver's seat, producing a ferocious crack that split the mirror in two and divided a tear-streaked Aben in half.

1966

Damn—It's Misery!

The sunshine of the seventh lunar month is the language of summer.

A sweltering, steamy, oily glint oozed from the asphalt, as shadows receded at noon to the bases of buildings. It was daytime, but there weren't many people out, and those who were seemed laughable, like animals forced to walk upright. A circle of boys with translucent heat rash on their bared chests were using nails to pick malt-like tar off the bubbling street surface. A carpenter in a bamboo hat pedaled toward them on a rickety bicycle as worn out as he was. An assortment of tools in his bag banged against each other, producing a rhythmic clang.

When he was a few yards away, he spotted the boys digging up tar, which upset him. He thought that maybe he'd scare them when he got closer, but he was too lazy to even shout as he rode by. He merely gave them a lackluster look and pedaled off, though the indignant flames of justice were still burning bright.

The sunshine grated on his nerves, like a mad musician belching noise from a golden trumpet. The sound of a real trumpet was audible, as blistering and fiery as the sun blazing down. It was coming from a long, seemingly endless funeral procession that meandered like a monster, crawling from the far end of the street. Led by musicians called "guides," the main part of the procession consisted of seventeen musical groups, which included a Western band with forty-six members from Zonglan she, a local opera troupe, a "ten-tone" troupe, and others. Everyone put on a good show the moment they entered the downtown area. With the cacophony from forty musical instruments, the procession resembled a beast that was howling from debilitating discomfort. Little by little, people came out to watch, their attention shifting from the boiling sun to the pandemonium.

Musicians were indispensable for any funeral procession, whether the family was rich or not. The poor could not afford other groups, but they had to at least pay for the "guides," who must be in the lead. The same held true for extravagant displays by a wealthy family. It was an age-old convention.

Two long, oversized bass suonas emitted discordant notes, accompanied by three other musicians. A small suona, the lead instrument, played an ancient tune, emotionlessly tossing moldy melodies into the sun like disinfectant. A man called Piggy Tail beat a small gong and a drum; another man called Doggie was in charge of cymbals.

The three percussion instruments accompanied the rhythm of the small suona in an indeterminate beat, requiring only mechanical movements—no thinking at all. So the musicians banged and clanged and drummed on, gawking at the gawkers. They even drew close enough to yell out an exchange:

"Hey, Doggie." The man raised his voice. "Doggie. Something wrong with your ears?"

"I heard you, Piggy Tail."

"I was just saying there are three funerals today."

"Wouldn't it be nice if they were held one a day, one after the other!"

"Yes."

"Louder. What did you just say?"

"I said that would give us one more place to enjoy a meal."

"People like us seem to hope for someone to die every day."

"What can we do about that?"

"What?"

"Maybe it'll be your turn soon."

"Ah-ren and the others got work today, too." Doggie had missed the jeering remark about him.

"But ours is the richest one."

"Did you just say I'll die soon?" It suddenly dawned on Doggie what his friend had said about him.

"Stop pretending you're deaf."

"Ha. You wish." A brief pause. "Who would play for me if I died?"

"There's only Ah-ren's band and ours in town, and they'd never play for anyone in ours."

"We'll do it ourselves, then. Who cares if no one plays the cymbals?"

"Do it ourselves? We'd die of shame!"

"Something's been bothering me. I think my lungs are getting weak."

"It's all in your head. You have a full voice when you talk."

"You think so?" He was doubtful. "What? I can't hear a thing today, not even the noise from our banging."

"It doesn't sound loud to me, either," Piggy Tail concurred. "Is it because of the Western band behind us?"

"Maybe it's the sun. I'm dying of thirst here."

DAMN—IT'S MISERY!

"Maybe we should stop talking. We'll be fine once we're off this street."

Piggy Tail and Doggie separated and walked with their heads down like prisoners who did not know one another. But it did not take long for Piggy Tail to edge back over to Doggie and say spiritedly: "I'm going to go look her up when I get my thirty NT today."

"What?"

"Damn. You want me to say it so loud that everyone can hear? Are you deaf?" Piggy Tail walked back to his position, feeling that the trip seemed especially long on this day.

With the streets packed with onlookers, no band, in fact not so much as a single musician, dared loaf on the job, no matter what they played, because of a decades-long competition between the Xipi and Fulu factions. This was the perfect time and place for them to put on a show in front of the crowd, a sentiment shared by just about every musician.

One-Eye, the leader of Piggy Tail's band, was the best suona player in town. No one had yet broken the record he'd set one summer evening at a thanksgiving ceremony in front of the Guardian Deity Temple, where he'd played for five hours straight. Several people had stayed near him, taking turns to wipe the sweat off his face and fan him. They were surrounded by a larger group of onlookers, some of whom bought bottles of rice liquor and red rice wine to keep him going. The rectangular table for sacrificial offerings was too small for all the bottles by the time he was into his record-breaking fourth hour of playing. The gong and drum beaters urged him on with an upbeat rhythm as a thick fog of firecracker smoke shrouded the ever-growing crowd. When One-Eye awoke the next day, he was bare-chested in a newly harvested rice field, cradling his suona and three empty bottles. It was an unforgettable experience, and an impressive feat that made him proud. Since then, he had enjoyed days of glory amid the circle of musicians, and he never passed up a chance to play his beloved instrument.

He walked ahead of more than thirty bands on this day as they filed down a street lined with onlookers, but he held the suona in his hand as he followed behind Piggy Tail, his head down. Right behind them came the Western band. The six young men, wearing ridiculous waiters' costumes and hats, were creating a din with their instruments. Being so close to them, One-Eye thought he would lose his mind over the noise; he hated those strange-looking instruments and the sounds they produced, and he loathed the swaggering young men. The only way to get away from them, he said to himself, was to die like the old man in the coffin.

Something didn't seem right to Doggie as he walked on and played his cymbals. He glanced at Piggy Tail, cocked his head, and put his cymbals up to his ears before walking up to the man.

"What do you hear?"

"What? Put your cymbals down so I can hear you."

"What?" Doggie couldn't hear Piggy Tail either, so he had to lower his cymbals.

"What did you just say?"

"I asked if you heard anything."

"What am I hearing?" Piggy Tail gave the question some thought. "Sunshine."

"I can't hear what we're playing."

"What can we do? There's so much going on. Just put on a show; we have to look serious for our thirty NT." Doggie placed the cymbals up to his ears again. "That's better." He took a few steps before walking back to Piggy Tail.

"Hey, Piggy Tail," he yelled, "I have a feeling. No, it's not really a feeling; it's something I'm hearing, like, um, like what?" He paused and blurted out, "I've got it. Misery. I'm feeling misery. I hear misery drowning out the sound of our instruments."

"That's crap. Misery." Belatedly Piggy Tail realized he'd been too loud, but he couldn't take it back. He looked back at One-Eye, who sometimes got upset when he and Doggie carried on a conversation along the way. One-Eye had heard him, and was shaken out of his languor by the last word, hit by the realization that what he, too, had been feeling all day was misery. He'd had a tough life, but today was the first time he hadn't enjoyed playing the suona. What better word to describe how he felt than misery? That was it. *It's misery*, he said to himself, while cursing silently. *Damn—it's misery*! He thought he'd had an epiphany, but he also felt helplessly confused. His mind wavered between the two extremes until he was mentally exhausted. The young coronet player behind him smugly compressed the smell from his stomach acid and digested food, and released it through his instrument to foul the air. Even the sun shining on the oily surface seemed to dance chaotically; it stung his eyes. One-Eye could not stop repeating his newly discovered curse, "Damn—it's misery."

***

The onlookers were talking about the display.
From a mother and son:
"Mom, do they have to pay for all the bands?"
"Of course they do, and they have to feed the musicians."
"Why?"
"Because the person who died was from a rich family."

"Who was he?"

"No idea."

"Look at the portrait, Mom. It's an old grandpa."

"Yes, I saw that. Don't shout and don't point."

Another exchange:

"Only Wangzai the butcher could have such a lavish funeral in our town."

"He was probably worth a million."

"No way! It has to be more than that. Two movie theaters, a paper mill—" The man went on, drawing the attention of those around him.

"Do I know the butcher, Mom?" the boy asked.

"Children are supposed to have ears but no mouth," his mother said as she listened in on the man.

"Wangzai was a tightwad all his life, but he had three concubines, plus other women outside marriage. Every one of them gave him several children."

An older man walked up and added: "Say what? Wangzai had eleven women, who gave him a grand total of forty-three children. They're all grown up now."

The man who had been holding forth stopped to listen to the newcomer.

"I know everything, since we worked together back behind the mountains when we were young. He was as strong as an ox back then. Once when Old Man Chen was building a house, he went to work as a hod carrier. He made a bet with the other workers about how much he could carry. He picked up the two heaviest women, who weighed at least fifty kilos each, and put them in bushel baskets. Then, with a bucket of water in one hand and two baskets on a pole over his shoulder, he climbed a ladder up onto the roof, not once but ten times. Seven workers handed over their wages that day. Later the two women bore him children."

"How did he get so rich?"

"He didn't do hard labor all his life, of course. He switched to the pig trade and did business with the Japanese army during the war. But I don't think that has anything to do with it. He just had a great sexual appetite." The old man smiled smugly.

The boy looked up at his mother and asked, "What's a great sexual appetite, Mom?" His mother quickly dragged him away.

The coffin moved quietly down the streets like a centipede, followed by more than a hundred mourning family members of all ages. The long line of female mourners with hemp head covers stood out from the group; they were muttering and sobbing, the only sign that someone had actually died.

"Where did all these relatives come from?" someone asked.

"From all over. When the family is rich—"

Once they were out of town, the lead mourner, who held one end of a mourning rope, walked the sobbing women toward some piles of cow dung; they avoided the obstacles and were able to keep their cloth shoes the white color of death. They never let up with their heartbreaking sobs.

Now that they were no longer in town, the "guides" band was the only one left to lead the coffin and family members to the gravesite. Yet One-Eye could not shake off the torment caused by the clamoring Western instruments. It took several tries before he managed to put the suona between his lips to play a few perfunctory notes, with beads of sweat prickling his forehead. The suona seemed harder to play than before. He had been holding it in his hand the whole day, and the grass-stalk reed had cracked under the harsh sun. There was a spare in his pocket, but he didn't feel like changing it.

Piggy Tail said to Doggie when they reached the cemetery, "We've earned half of the thirty NT."

"Are you really going to spend it on Baggy Breasts?"

"She needs money and I need her. What's wrong with that?"

"But—"

"I know. You discovered misery today, didn't you? Well you can have all the misery you want."

"I don't think I should be talking to you about this now."

"That's how you discovered misery."

The coffin was lowered into the ground. Under the punishing sun, the bell in the Taoist priest's hand seemed to mock the cycle of human life and death: those born first died first; those born later died later; those dying first were reborn first; those dying later were reborn later. The family of the deceased circled the new grave three times, while a pile of paper money for the underworld burned off the connection between the living and the dead. One-Eye, who was standing to the side, picked that moment to wail; throwing his suona to the ground and stomping on it, he mumbled and cursed, "Damn—it's misery!"

Sweat, snot, and a single line of tears came together to form the sad sight of a failure, stunning everyone; even the bell could not find anything to mock.

Everyone in the family of the deceased was unnerved, as they mistook One-Eye for another relative wanting his share of the inheritance. In startled and nervous voices they asked each other, "Who's his mother?"

"I don't know, but listen. Doesn't it sound like he's saying 'Damn—it's, misery'?"

1967

A Headless Wasp

It was nearing dusk in the summertime, and a royal palm extended its shadow into the intersection where evening would appear. It would lie peacefully on the grass, quietly waiting for evening to descend upon its arrow-like trunk as if gliding down a slide. But it would be a while before the moment arrived.

On Sunday he spent his daytime hours at the library, burying his head in materials he needed in order to write an essay that would become a masterpiece (at least he thought so): "Humans, Apes, and Voting Rights." He would soon begin his first summer break since entering college. Over the past few days, thanks to the essay, he had come to realize that he was a borderline genius. He regretted having discovered so late in the game that he had aptitude and potential in the subject of political science. He could recall the first few preferred majors he'd picked prior to the college entrance exam, but not where he had put down political science in the school of law.

The librarian had turned on the lights, but he was sitting by a window and would have preferred that they not be on at the moment. Laying down his pen, he let his tired eyes roam over every word of the draft he'd written so far. At some point he picked up his pen to scratch out or add a few words, looking mightily pleased with himself.

He had been tearfully disappointed that night a year earlier when he'd heard over the radio that his name was included on the list of students admitted to the political science department at K University. Instead of feeling the excitement common among freshmen, he was still lamenting the outcome after school started. What really galled him was that his old high school friends would not stop calling him "Prime Minister." He had talked himself into enrolling because he wasn't confident enough to take the exam for the fourth time. But in fact, after several visits home since becoming a college student, he'd been encouraged by the neighborhood elders, who thought highly of him because so few from their small village had made it that far. At some point, the elders, who liked to congregate at the temple to shoot the breeze, started saying that, given what he was studying, he would be the prime minister one day.

He was tired and hungry, but it would be at least another thirty minutes before mealtime, so he left the library and found the royal palm. Leaning against the trunk, he was entirely in its shade. Someone stuck his head out from behind a hibiscus bush across the way when he was about to close his eyes and rest.

"Hey, Prime Minister."

He had gotten used to the nickname.

"Hey, Sex Maniac," he greeted his friend Jian Jinmu, a classmate whose interest in drawing had earned him the nickname.

"How's the doctoral thesis coming along?"

"It'll be done soon. I'll have a third of it finished by the end of summer break."

"And what's your conclusion? Should apes have voting rights?"

"Yes, but that's not the point. The point is, any member of a society has the right to vote in his own district as long as he has a certain level of cognitive ability. Hence, a bridge or a public toilet could vote for someone appropriate if it could think, because it would know what makes a sturdy bridge or a sanitary toilet."

"Ha! I've spotted a talent of yours that even you don't know about."

"What's that?" He was delighted.

"I think you'd be much more successful than Aesop if you decided to write fables. He only personified animals, but you've gone beyond him by anthropomorphizing public toilets. A 1960s fabulist does indeed differ from one of two thousand years ago."

"Hear me out, Sex Maniac," he continued patiently. "That was just a metaphor. But I don't have time to explain and you don't have time to listen, so just wait to read my essay."

"To take your high-flung idea a step further, I'd say that the zoo animals should have a better life during election season."

"If they could think, they'd have the right to demand fairness from society."

"Fairness? Letting them return to nature would be true fairness."

"We're digressing, and we'll just be wasting our time if we continue to argue along this line. But let me add a bit to what you just said. They would be entitled to vote if, after returning to nature, they could think like humans who had voting privileges, because then they would be influential members of society." Prime Minister's patience was ebbing. "But actually these creatures will never have the capacity for complex thought. On the other hand, a child should be able to vote as long as his mind is mature and he is mentally older than his biological age. Conversely, many people have a simple, immature mind even when they reach voting age. Ai! I have lots of details and analysis; you'll have to wait to read my essay."

"I am so lucky and deeply honored," his friend said mockingly. "When will you have time for me to draw you? That could bring me eternal fame, you know."

"Let's forget about me. Are you really going to take the exam for a fine arts major this summer? Wouldn't that be a waste?"

"You're a prime minister and I'm a sex maniac, so how would that be a waste? Besides, I'm more confident this year. I flunked the technical part last year, but I've improved on that considerably."

"How about the academic subjects? Can you still handle them?"

"Those are easy. I'll have no problem getting into the fine arts department based upon my results from testing into poli-sci." His friend paused. "If I'm such a dimwit and fail again, I can always come back to poli-sci and study drawing in my spare time. It would be a legitimate pastime, on the one hand, and on the other hand it could come in handy." He wore a smug, cryptic smile.

"I'm not going anywhere." He sounded firm, with no hint of regret.

"Sure, you have to stay to finish your doctoral thesis. Maybe you can even get driver's licenses for your apes." His friend laughed. Since that sort of sardonic laughter had always gotten on his nerves, he replied with obvious irritation, "Sex Maniac, I take this essay seriously, and I don't want to hear you joke about it again."

"Sorry, so sorry. I was being serious, but you took it as a joke. Well, we won't talk about apes again, then, your kind of apes." The repeated mention of apes, along with the stress, was clearly meant to annoy him. With a wave and a "bye-bye," his friend walked off with his sketchpad.

He felt miserable, and all his unhappiness surfaced. Sex Maniac wasn't the only person who mocked him; others in his class had said he was old before his time when they heard he was already writing his senior thesis. Some had fun at his expense by arguing and ganging up on him, until he was alone. Once he got so worked up by the taunts he jumped onto a desk and shouted, "I get it now. You're talking about apes that eat bananas. You eat bananas, too, but you're no match for those apes when it comes to eating bananas. Humans' sorrow stems from their arrogance."

He lit a cigarette and leaned back against the tree to relax his muscles, but before he had taken a second puff, he felt a powerful itch on his neck. He reached back to scratch himself, but when he turned to look, he saw that he was leaning against a procession of ants climbing up the trunk. A closer look showed that there were a couple dozen of them carrying a struggling creature up from the grass. Curious, he picked up the ants' prey and laid it on his notebook. It was a headless wasp, waging its last fight. He pinched off the few ants still holding on to the wasp. The wasp calmed down and planted its six legs squarely on his notebook, as if it still had a head. That puzzled him. There were plenty of wasps in the hillside orchards back home, but this was the first headless one he'd seen. How could it survive without a head? A human being couldn't. Which meant that the human head is in charge of life, but a wasp's head is not; a human head can think, but a wasp's head can't. Then he was reminded of people who can survive without a head, people like wasps, with no need for a head to think. He seemed to have stumbled upon something from the headless wasp, a thought that so elated him that he continued his examination.

He held up the notebook at a forty-five-degree angle; the wasp remained motionless. Then he stood the notebook at a ninety-degree angle; still no movement from the wasp. When he turned the notebook upside down, the wasp continued to hold on to the paper fiber with its four front legs, only letting go with the two longer ones in the rear. *Is that an instinctual action, to hold on with four legs?* he asked himself. *Or is it willpower? But where does the willpower come from now that it has lost its head? Does it mean that a wasp has willpower when its head is intact? What would happen if this one had its head? It would fly away. Or maybe it wouldn't; it might fall, a worse fate than when it had a head. How different is that from humans under similar circumstances? Hard to say. Every person is different—some drastically, while others might be much like a wasp.* By then he was trapped in weariness, as a jumble of thoughts besieged his mind. He couldn't let go, but it distressed him to continue; his head felt like it might explode.

Once he understood that the wasp's head was not in total charge of its life, curiosity spurred him on to further exploration. He put the insect upside down on the notebook; it quickly flipped over and stood up, now looking alert and guarded. Which meant that its head did not control its balance. He blew cigarette smoke at it, making it writhe in pain and proving that its head had nothing to do with the senses of taste or smell, either. When he poked its tail with a match, the insect swung its stinger back and forth, searching for its attacker. Self-defense was unrelated to the head.

The headless wasp could even take a few steps forward. In the end, he tossed the headless insect into the air. It couldn't fly, but when it got closer to the ground, it landed lightly on the grass in a gliding motion. Repeated experiments yielded the same results. He began to wonder about the importance of the head to a wasp. By chance he spotted three ants from the original formation carrying something down from the tree. He was amazed when he picked it up, for it was a wasp's head; it must have belonged to the insect in his hand, though he could not be sure. The head had no life in it, and he could put it anywhere without getting a reaction.

A girl from his class named Gao Qiufeng sneaked up on him and said, "I was intrigued by the look on your face, even from a distance."

"Look here. This headless wasp caught my attention, so I've been watching it."

"Because it's headless?"

"Oh, no." He asked her to sit beside him so he could tell her all about his observations and conclusions. "Look, this is its head and here's its body. Which side would you take?'

She smiled without answering, to his disappointment.

"Maybe your non-answer is an answer itself; either you don't think there is a side to take or you feel sorry for the whole insect. But which side do you feel bad for when the head is separated from the body? Girls usually are more compassionate." He added the last phrase in hopes of getting a response.

"You obviously want an answer from me, don't you?" She was coy.

"Uh-huh—"

"I feel sorry for you."

"What do you mean?"

"I feel sorry for you for feeling sorry for a part of a wasp."

"You mean I've failed by asking such a vague and abstract question? So, with humans, which do you feel sorrier about, the death of an idiot or a normal person?"

"What does that have to do with wasps?" She was confused. "To tell you the truth, Prime Minister, you're too serious when you talk. Oh, yes, I have to apologize for not being able to fill out the questionnaire you gave us last week. Also, I'll give you back your books in a few days."

"It doesn't matter. If you're too busy to fill it out, it's still better than the ones who gave ridiculous answers. And don't worry about the books."

"But I have to. I may not come back next semester."

"Won't that be a pity."

"I never liked poli-sci."

"Me either, but I'm staying. I'm not changing my major."

He continued his exploration after she left by putting the head against the body, but the headless insect kept backing off. *How come? Don't you miss it?* he asked silently. *You fought like hell when your head was being lopped off, but you don't want it now that it's gone. Is that it? Why couldn't she have some thoughts about a headless wasp? Despite a lack of thoughts, views of their own, or ideals, with no willpower or wisdom, people continue to live.* What else did he want to learn from the insect? Whatever it was, it would only baffle him more. Suddenly bored, he flicked the insect and its head off his notebook.

"This is obviously a subject for entomology majors," he mumbled with a smile.

The shadow of the royal palm had stretched out farther. He compared the headless wasp to people he knew, people like Liao

Meijin, his teaching-college girlfriend. He recalled their date the previous week. She had complained when they walked out of the theater after watching *A Talented Scholar and a Pretty Lady*. "You embarrassed me when you laughed like that. You at least should have thought about me sitting beside you. But no, you kept laughing even when the movie was over and the lights came on. Only a sicko would do that. Do you know what other people say about you?"

"You've already told me, and I agreed with you. Of course I can't ask you to be like me, but you don't understand why I found the movie silly."

"Who doesn't know it's a silly movie?"

"You."

"Ridiculous. You're the only one who's smart enough, the only one with a sense of humor."

"I don't want to argue with you. The reason you're mad at me is that I was the only person still laughing after the lights came on, so everyone was looking at me and at you, too, and you were embarrassed. Am I right? But it was really a silly movie. Don't you see how shallow and puerile some American movies can be? Can you imagine a woman, in particular, asking other people if she had sex the night before? She was actually a virgin! If it were you—"

The last comment made Meijin so mad she jumped onto a three wheeler and rode off. He wanted to explain himself, but she refused to see him. Now he wondered why he wasn't bothered when she gave him the cold shoulder. Straightening out his legs, he plucked a blade of grass and put it in his mouth. *Do I love her?* he asked himself. *I do like her pretty face, but I never think about anything else. I like her face, but does that mean I have to accept all her shortcomings, like her bourgeois, arrogant, rigid, and old-fashioned attitude? But it's pretty much out of my hands, since she's the only one who will go out with me.* Just for fun, he began to create a composite image of his ideal woman: Meijin's face, Gao Qiufeng's breasts and buttocks, the fair skin of the pharmacy owner, and the legs of a woman he'd spotted once on a train home. He was so tickled by his collage that he began to laugh. Unlike wasps, humans must be treated as a whole and not taken apart to inspect. If you want a saint's soul, you must accept the scabs on his body. A sudden spasm in his back made him abruptly change position and lose his train of thought.

Evening slowly descended. He jumped to his feet and hurried off, leaving his notebook and the draft essay behind. It was still light enough to see the signature on the cover:

First-year, Poli-sci, Huang Ah-tu.

1967

The Gong

PROLOGUE

Han Qinzai had not beaten his gong for quite some time now, probably eight or nine months, maybe as long as a year. He wasn't sure himself. He knew only that it had been a long, long time. Whenever this fact crossed his mind a great anger filled him: here he was, the only remaining practitioner of the unique profession of gong beating, and no one ever came to commission his services. By the time he realized what was happening, it was too late to do anything about it. The brass gong upon which his carefree existence had depended for more than half a lifetime now suddenly lay there like something that had been frightened out of its wits, resembling the vacantly opened mouth of a mute. It had lain upside down under his bamboo bed since his last job, serving as a catchall.

That doesn't mean that there were no longer any lost children in the town, or that there were no more calls for the Buddhist faithful to offer prayerful thanks on the various temple days, or that the need no longer existed to announce publicly for the people to pay their taxes, or that smallpox vaccinations for the children were no longer given. But now these announcements were the responsibility of a young man who pedaled his loudspeaker-equipped pedicab up and down the streets. This sight produced more than just loathing in Han Qinzai; there was also an ineffable, persistent pain that gripped his heart. There was something terribly unfitting, he thought, about having such a bizarre contraption anywhere in his little town. The appearance of this *thing* would destroy the town's social fabric—it represented an extreme absurdity.

Back in the days when Han Qinzai's gong was still in use, every third day witnessed a minor event, every fifth a major one. So among the town's old bachelors, known locally as arhat vagrants, he drank wine more frequently than all the others, and sometimes when he had a little more money, he'd even splurge and buy some of the more expensive Shaoxing wine. And in the matter of names, why, even among people of distinction there was no one whose name carried the weight of Han Qinzai's. You had only to say the three words, *han—qin—zai*, and anyone—literate or illiterate, man, woman, or child—would know at once of whom you spoke. But were you to mention the mayor of the town, Brother Futong, or refer to him even more precisely as the old doctor's grandson, well, old doctor's grandson or not, there were no guarantees that everyone would recognize his name. Yes, in those days Han Qinzai could truly lay claim to both fame and fortune.

But ever since the pedicab with the loudspeaker had come to town, quickly monopolizing the public announcement business, the group of arhat vagrants who congregated beneath the *kadang* tree opposite the coffin shop at Southgate was increased by the addition of one Han Qinzai. In order to secure his position in the group, he had methodically and deliberately planned his every move, as though it were an intricate game of chess. For now that fortune was missing from his life, he was left with only his reputation. It was important not only to win this game but to preserve face as well. In his heart he knew that he was going to hang around there one way or the other, and that sooner or later he would have his place beneath the kadang tree. *But I, Han Qinzai, am not that stupid! I still want to take my place in society with other people!* He knew that it was important for a man to play a role in society. So whenever he had the feeling that he somehow belonged, no matter to what depths his spirits had sunk, they would be given a momentary boost.

THE GHOST SIGHTING

By now a considerable amount of time had passed since Han Qinzai had last beaten his gong. He had lost his source of income, and although there was only himself to look after, even a marginal existence was proving difficult. He could do without wine, but not without food!

Of the ten or so roads in town, only two or three did not give Han Qinzai a sinking feeling as he walked down them, for on the other roads were general stores where he had run up bills for wine and tobacco. Times being what they were, he felt as if he were being wedged into a long, deep fissure in which he was powerless to budge an inch. For days he had thought of little else, and he could come up with no more practical plan than to squeeze himself into the group in the shade of the kadang tree opposite the coffin shop.

Bright and early every morning he went over to the yam patch in the Alishi area alongside the stream to steal some yams. By now he was sick of the things; in fact, he had recently been bothered by indigestion, which caused his throat to grow parched and hoarse. As he saw it, the shade of the kadang tree opposite the coffin shop offered his only hope for survival. Once made, the decision to go there gained the force of a mandate.

With a jolt he sat up in bed. The bright light shining in through the opening of the air-raid shelter at that moment brought with it revitalized hope. In the brief moment that his gaze was fixed straight ahead, he felt as light as a feather and imagined himself to be flying away on the rays of light.

Before walking out of the little park, he washed his face at the fountain, then went over in his mind once more the route he had planned: leaving the park, he'd cut across the Lans' vegetable garden via the narrow, dark path. No problems there. When he reached the Utopia Hospital, he'd skirt around the marketplace, taking the alleyway in back of the Revival Movie house. He'd be careful to avoid the metal workshop, for it was likely that Stony and the others, whose shop was nearby, might be around. Han Qinzai made a mental calculation: this route would certainly take him to Northgate, to the train station. He'd walk along the canal, and from there it would be best to cut across the Youying Public School playground. Once he'd reached the train station, he'd cross the tracks and take Ashushe Road, which would put him on the outskirts of town. *If I run into any of them out there, I'm dead meat.* From there he'd follow the road back to the Buddhist temple at Point Sixteen, cross back over the tracks to the west side of town, then turn south at the rice shop beneath the melia tree.

When his thoughts reached this point, he sucked in his breath. *Wa! That road would take me out of the area altogether, wouldn't it?* He smiled. Using such a roundabout route just to get to Southgate was like taking off your pants to fart!

He scratched his head hard and twisted his mouth. It suddenly dawned on him that he had become very clever. Clever? Crafty was more like it. *Well, since crafty is the same as clever, isn't clever the same as crafty?* He gleefully embraced this sense of self-respect, then crisply spat on the ground. He squinted into the sky to locate the sun's position: it was slanting above his head. He felt terribly hungry. It must be past noon already, he thought, probably after two o'clock.

There was a breach in the northern wall of the park, which most people called "the dog door" but which people who actually made use of it called "the side entrance." There were but three formal entrances to the park; this breach in the wall, the "dog door" or "side entrance", had been opened up by the bean curd makers at Red Tile Shelter as a shortcut for their trips to the marketplace. With the exception of their early-morning passages, few people took advantage of this shortcut. That was because in order to make your way through Mr. Lan's vegetable patch, you had to walk along a narrow, fenced-in lane in the middle of which were two manure pits hidden in the shade of a large banyan tree. From that very tree, one of the Lan family women had hanged herself one day, and the townspeople were convinced that her ghost often appeared there.

Han Qinzai's heart was heavy as he drew up to the breach in the wall. For some reason an old town saying came to him: "The hungry ghost is king of the ghosts, the full-bellied ghost is startled by the winds." And yet he grew bold, repeating this saying aloud over and over as if it were a chant of exorcism. As he neared the manure pits, several papaya trees nearby suddenly attracted his eyes. Three or four huge papayas hung from one of the trees, their stems a pale yellow. What a waste, he thought as he looked carefully around him, forgetting all about his chant. Standing on the edge of one of the manure pits on his tiptoes, he reached out to gauge the distance to the nearest papaya. If the pit weren't in the way, he'd only have to knock the papaya to the ground with a piece of bamboo fencing. But, stymied by the manure pit, he looked around until his gaze stopped at the bamboo fence: a piece of fencing that had fallen over until its tip was touching the ground gave him an idea. He walked over and unhooked the fence wire, thinking as he did so that once he'd knocked down the papaya, he could use the bamboo for a cook fire. The butterfly bushes alongside the fence were as tall as a man. Closer to the ground there was a thick undergrowth of canna plants, and this wild growth of wattle had already replaced the original bamboo fence—there was no evidence of any repair work by the owner of the rotting fence. Han Qinzai removed the last coil of wire, then happily grabbed the bamboo in both hands; but just as he was about to reach out and knock down the papaya, he sensed that someone was coming. Quickly throwing the bamboo into the bushes, he ran to the edge of the manure pit, pulled down his trousers, and squatted there to wait and see what the person would do. Nothing happened.

That's strange, I'm sure I heard someone coming. Why can't I see anyone? Could he have spotted me first? Maybe he's lying in wait to nab me. To hell with him. I'll just squat here a while longer and see what happens. After all, it's no crime to come here and relieve myself. He chuckled to himself. *If I don't get my hands on the papaya, that'll make five meals I've missed, and soon there won't be anything left to relieve myself of. Shit!* He laughed again.

His thoughts returned to a few days earlier, when he'd gone to steal yams at Alishi. The owner had discovered him just as he was about to dig into the patch. The man had started yelling as he ran over from some distance away, so Han Qinzai had quickly dropped his trousers and squatted there casually without moving. When the other man was no more than ten steps away, Han Qinzai really let him have it:

"What's this? You coming over here to eat shit? How dare you accuse me of being a thief! Wait till I'm finished here, then if I don't rub your face in my shit, you'll be getting off easy! Anyone who accuses someone of being a thief doesn't know right from wrong. What kind of person do you think I am? How dare you!"

The young farmer had answered doubtfully, almost apologetically, "What's the big idea of coming here to crap?"

"What's that? Are you complaining because I deliver it right to your door? Don't you go into town every morning before sunrise to pick the stuff up?" The young man had walked off without another word, and Han Qinzai had left laden with booty.

At this point his mind was brought back to the present; he carefully sized up the situation. Still no sounds of anyone drawing near, and it struck him that whoever was trying to nab him might just be very crafty. *All right, I'll squat here a little longer.* He laughed to himself again. This was all very funny to him. *There's nothing easier than getting the best of one of these hicks. The people who plant yams in Alishi just serve them right up to people like me. If you get caught, all you have to say is that you're from the Fulunzai area, and that we're all members of the same group. Then the man who's caught you will say politely, "These out here are no good. I've got better ones in the house." Then he'll take you over and let you help yourself to as much as a hundred catties if you want that much, and might even have you stay for dinner. Naturally, if you tell him you belong to one of the other groups from Ashushe, he'll beat the hell out of you on the spot.* Um! He heaved a long sigh. In a matter of a few years a whole new era had begun.

He knew he couldn't squat there much longer, since his legs were cramping, so he stood up and looked around, concerned that he wouldn't be able to see if there was anyone else in the patch. He parted the clumps of butterfly bushes in several places, taking care not to let down his guard. Then he hit upon a plan. He called out, not too loudly, "Someone's stealing papayas! Someone's stealing papayas!" That way, if anyone came asking questions, he could say that he'd seen a couple of kids but they must have run away. He waited a moment—no response. Now he knew there was no one around. So, picking up the bamboo fencing from the butterfly bushes where he'd thrown it, he tried to knock down the papaya. But he'd grown so weak from hunger that he couldn't handle the eight- or nine-foot-long bamboo, which kept whipping back and forth in the air. The harder he tried to hit the papaya, the worse his aim became, until he began to grow anxious and frustrated.

As he saw it, there were some things that required a certain amount of cursing if they were to be done properly. "You fucking thing, you!" A burst of effort, and he actually hit it. But the big papaya he had in his sights fell with a thud onto a layer of dried excrement atop the manure pit and began to sink slowly to the bottom. Han Qinzai stood there transfixed, like a man who has just parted with his lover, following the sinking papaya with his eyes. He swallowed a couple of times, hoping somehow to lessen the pangs of hunger.

When the papaya that had so tantalized him sank to just beyond the halfway point, the bumps and hollows of the skin and its general shape made it look like a human head, with eyes, a nose, even a mouth. Han Qinzai's heart raced violently, and he blinked hard to clear his vision. Suddenly the heavy end of the papaya sank below the surface as the lighter end bobbed straight up. Terrified, Han Qinzai fled down the lane, screaming out to Heaven, earth, and mother. Some people on the road adjoining this darkened lane were startled by his shouts and cursed him:

"Damn you, have you seen a ghost or something?"

"Yes... Yes, I... I saw a ghost!" Han Qinzai stammered in response. On that June harvest day, Han Qinzai was actually shivering uncontrollably.

Han Qinzai had always been a believer in ghosts and spirits, and this experience caused his superstitions to become more deeply entrenched. Seeing a ghost is a very unlucky omen, he thought to himself, especially in broad daylight. He temporarily postponed his plan to go over to the kadang tree opposite the coffin shop at Southgate. To solve his food problems of the next few days, no matter how uncomfortable his stomach was, he'd have to go beg yams from someone at Alishi to stay his hunger.

Beginning on the day Han Qinzai saw the apparition, the ghost of the girl named Lan, which had been all but forgotten by the townsfolk, began once again nightly to infiltrate the minds of those most fearful of ghosts, the town's children in particular.

Since Han Qinzai had seen the ghost, over the next few days

many idlers came to the air-raid shelter when they were in the park to ask him about it. He never wearied of giving an animated account, usually winding up by painting a heroic picture of himself. He naturally avoided any mention of stealing papayas. Some of the children hung around the air-raid shelter all day long listening to him answer people's questions and describe his encounter with the ghost; they never got tired of hearing about it. They'd ask all sorts of questions about ghosts.

"Was her tongue this long?" a child asked, sticking his tongue out as far as it would go.

"That's nothing!" Han Qinzai put his hand down on a level with his navel and said, "It came down to here, all the way to her belly button."

"Wa!" The child's face grew pinched and small, though his staring eyes were larger than ever.

"Her... her..." Another child wanted to ask something. "Whew! I'm afraid to say it."

"He wants to know what the ghost's eyes looked like," one of the other kids said.

"Her eyes! Wa! They were this big." He made circles with his fingers the size of eyeglass lenses. "But I couldn't see the pupils—the eyes were all white, with blood-red lines running through them."

"When she walked, did she float above the ground?"

"Of course she did!"

"Were her nails long?"

"This long. And there was poison on every one of them. Any place they touched a person it turned to blood."

"Aiyo! Weren't you scared?"

"Me? Not too scared. If I had been, she'd have snatched me

away then and there!"

Thus earning looks of respect and admiration from the children around him, Han Qinzai grew more and more expansive, eventually convincing himself that everything he said was true. Once he'd gained the respect of these children, for several days they went out and fetched the firewood and water he needed. As a result, he experienced an incomprehensible sensation of floating in air.

A BLADE OF GRASS, A DROP OF DEW

A week or so later his stomach had reached the point where it could not tolerate another sliver of yam. He looked down at the pile of yams on the floor by the head of his bed—there were enough left for three or four more days—then, with his hands on his hips, he stepped toward them, touched them with his toe, and said, "So that's the way it is. I always thought the Alishi folks were generous people who would let me take all I wanted."

He thought back to his sighting of the ghost—it had already been eight or nine days at least. By now the bad luck should have vanished, which ought to forestall any calamities for the time being. He could no longer postpone his plan to go over to the spot opposite the coffin shop at Southgate.

After waking from a somewhat troubled nap, he sat in bed and dully scratched himself all over. He was fully awake by the time he was scratching his head with both hands, thinking of the one important matter he had not yet taken care of.

With extreme caution he took a circuitous route to the Southgate area. When he reached the Buddhist temple on Ashushe

Road, where there was a small general store in front of which a pot of tea had been placed for thirsty passersby, Han Qinzai walked quickly over to it. Actually, what had aroused his interest was the tobacco and wine sign hanging under the eaves. He couldn't actually read the words, but he knew that any store that displayed one of those round lacquered metal signs was a tobacco and wine outlet. He walked up to the place, poured a glass of tea, and held it in his hands. As he drank the tea, his eyes scanned the inside of the store. He noticed an old man dozing behind the counter, who raised his head as Han Qinzai walked up closer to get a better look.

"Hey, boss, this is quite some tea you have here."

He took another swallow. "It must be from Wulaokeng."

The old man smiled and said, "How could we have tea as fine as that? We grow this in our own tea garden."

"Really?" He drank another mouthful. "Where is this tea garden of yours?"

"Over on Thirteen Hills."

"Aha! Wulaokeng is just on the other side of Thirteen Hills. I'm an expert where tea is concerned." He took another drink. "Not bad, not bad at all. This tea is every bit as good as Wulaokeng." As he was talking, he walked into the store and plopped down on the wooden bench in front of the counter.

Hearing someone praise the tea he had set out for pedestrians, the old man was naturally quite elated.

Han Qinzai had spotted the pastries inside the glass-enclosed counter right off; the sight of them made his stomach growl. But each time he was about to ask the old man to let him buy something on the cuff, he stopped himself. The opportune moment hadn't yet arrived, he calculated, so he racked his brain for something to chat with the old man about.

"Shit!" Han Qinzai cursed out of the blue. Before the old man even had time to puzzle over this, Han Qinzai continued, "I saw a ghost a few days ago. My bad luck!"

"Yeah, I heard people talking about it. They said it was at the Lans' vegetable patch."

"That's the goddamn place!"

"That's always been a bad piece of land."

"I know. But I had something important to do that day, so I cut across there to save some time."

"I heard it happened in broad daylight."

"That's exactly when it happened! Right after lunch."

"Wa! That was some evil ghost to actually appear in the daytime."

"You're right there. Who'd have thought it?" Han Qinzai tilted his head back and drained the cup of tea. "I think I'll have another cup," he said as he rose to walk outside.

"A connoisseur like you should drink some of this—it's hot." The old man reached over beside his chair, took a pot of steaming hot tea from a carrying case, and poured some into Han Qinzai's cup.

"Oh, that's great. Lucky, lucky me. Whoa! That's fine, that's fine. It's full."

"Think nothing of it, and if you want more, just help yourself."

"That's plenty." Seeing the happy expression on the old man's face, he added, "It's always best to have a little pastry to go with fine tea like this."

"That's for sure. These pastries here are real fresh—delivered today."

"I've never done any business in this store of yours—too far from where I live. How about the Prosperity and Longevity stores in town—do you know them?"

"Of course I know them! But how could a little store like mine compare with the likes of them?"

"I get all my tobacco and wine and other things at those places. If it's not Prosperity, then it's Longevity. I buy on credit, then pay them off all at once. The day before yesterday I paid off a pretty big bill at Longevity."

The old man walked over to the counter, opened the glass case, and asked, "How many do you want? Round ones or twists?"

"Forget it. I'll go over to the Buddhist temple in a moment and collect a debt, then I'll come back."

"We're not strangers. Why don't you eat some first?"

Han Qinzai thought about politely refusing again as a disarming gesture, but to his own surprise he blurted out, "Okay, then give me four of the round ones." He was feeling a little guilty, but when he saw how willing the old man was to extend him credit he felt relieved.

All together he ate six of the round pastries and drank three cups of tea. He was feeling considerably more comfortable now. But he still wasn't completely satisfied—he longed for a smoke. Looking up at the cigarettes in the glass case behind the counter, he turned his thoughts to ways to keep the conversation going.

"It's been a long time since I saw you beating your gong," the old man said.

This threw Han Qinzai into such a panic that he could only mutter in response. If he couldn't steer the conversation in the direction he wanted, it would be very hard to have his way with the old man. He put the empty cup up to his lips and pretended to be drinking so he wouldn't have to answer at once. Suddenly he knew what to say.

"Tsk, tsk. So you want to know about me and the gong, eh?"

"You haven't beaten it for some time, have you?"

"No, I still do it, but it's awfully tiring. Sometimes I get a youngster to do the shouting for me, but at other times I do it all myself."

"I haven't seen you out there for a long time."

"I was out just the day before yesterday."

"Not over here."

Han Qinzai smiled, then said, "It wasn't good news, so I knocked off after a while."

"What was the job?"

"Taxes!" He smiled again. "If it had been good news, I'd have made sure everyone heard it." Then he added the punch line. "Say, boss, how about giving me a couple of packs of Long Life cigarettes? I'll pay for it all later."

The old man took a look at his cigarette supply. "How about a pack of Red Paradise instead? I only have two packs of Long Life left."

"I'm used to smoking Long Life. It won't make any difference, since I'll probably be back to pay you for them in a little while."

Han Qinzai's belly was now full and his pockets were stuffed with two packs of Long Life cigarettes. Everything's going right today, he thought. He headed toward the Buddhist temple, figuring that within a quarter of an hour or so he'd reach Southgate. He rubbed his slightly protruding belly, now stuffed with pastries and several cups of tea. Looking off toward the horizon, he mumbled to himself, "Hai! The old saying is right on the mark: 'A blade of grass, a drop of dew.' Damned if it isn't true—'A blade of grass, a drop of dew.'" He very cautiously puffed on the cigarette, which was now as short as it was ever going to get, as though he were engaged in a parting kiss. When he could no longer put off throwing it away, he pinched the tiny remainder between his fingers, then looked down at it; there was no way he could put it back to his lips. He blew out the last puff of smoke. Totally relaxed and at ease, he felt like leaping into the clouds and flying over to Southgate.

THE NARROW ROAD

Usually there were eight or nine arhat vagrants squatting beneath the kadang tree opposite the coffin shop. Whenever a family of mourners came to buy a coffin, these vagrants would go over to hang around and assist the family in its mourning duties. They'd do things like carry banners and floral wreaths in the funeral procession, or whatever other sundry jobs were required. This would earn them the right to join the funeral banquet for two or three days, and sometimes even a week or so. They'd also divide up a little pocket money. These old vagrants were men with no families or involvements who for a long time had passed their days squatting under the kadang tree. There was even a system of rights and privileges that had been established within their small circle. Naturally they were well versed on the quality of coffins. If, for instance, two grieving families came to buy lacquered coffins at the same time, one made of cedar, the other made of the more expensive cypress, they'd immediately catch the scent of the cypress and fall in behind it. If it was a wealthy family, there was always a great show of pageantry and the possibility of food and drink for more than a week, plus a substantial amount of pocket money. But once in a while there was an exception. Han Qinzai knew just about everything there was to know about these men, so when he lost his job of beating the gong, it was only natural that he should decide to throw in his lot with them.

Only a stretch of road separated the coffin shop from the vacant lot beneath the kadang tree. The rhythmic, even sounds of the axe chopping and the two-man saw being pulled by the two coffin shop apprentices lulled the group of men into a mid-day nap. Some of the old vagrants slept soundly in the shade of the tree, their faces covered with wide rain hats; they looked like the red and gray stones of the chess game they played before their nap, which were scattered freely about. Others sat in their customary places chewing the fat with one another. But their conversations were so lacking in compatibility that it often seemed like each of them was talking to himself. Every once in a while a truck would roar past them down the road, causing them to reflect that there was a big world out there, one they had no desire to belong to.

Han Qinzai walked up to a spot beneath the tree, where he saw this group of carefree vagrants spread out in all positions—seated, standing, supine. He was struck by a sense of disappointment as he realized that if he joined up with them, one of those scattered bodies would be his. He'd been able to conjure up visions of what their lives were like, but seeing them now dealt a blow to his self-respect. He had to strain to think of any redeeming features they might have. Finally, pulling out one of his packs of Long Life cigarettes, he walked over to the man called Scabby Head, who was having a smoke, to bum a light. He made a point of showing off the pack of Long Lifes, which elicited from the sleepy vagrants wide-eyed looks of envy—the cigarettes had captured their attention. He handed the matches back to Scabby Head, then offered cigarettes to the others. His heart was pained to see four or five hands quickly stretch out toward him.

"How come we haven't seen you out with your gong?" Scabby Head asked him.

"That's right, it's been a long time," someone else commented.

"I quit," Han Qinzai answered nonchalantly, blowing out a puff of smoke. "Beating a gong doesn't interest me anymore."

But someone else asked in a doubting tone, "Don't you mean the loudspeaker pedicab took your rice bowl away?"

This comment grated on his ears. He glared at the man who'd said it; seeing that the man was smoking the cigarette he had given him, he felt even worse. Wanting to squelch the effect of the man's statement, he said contemptuously:

"What's so great about a grotesque thing like that? It just so happens that old Han Qinzai here didn't want to beat the gong anymore, and that other guy just picked up the slack. Shit! A lot of people are under the impression that this old hand, Han Qinzai here, had his rice bowl smashed by some young punk!"

"Actually, beating a gong's not a bad job."

"Not bad?" His brow furrowed as he took a deep puff on his cigarette. "How would you know? You've never done it. Sometimes I was out there so long I lost my voice and my legs were sore for days. But all that wouldn't have mattered if they'd always paid me for my efforts! Wouldn't that make your blood boil! Good, you say? It's about as good as a fart, that's how good it is!"

"Are there really deadbeats like that?"

Han Qinzai saw that several of the old vagrants smoking his cigarettes were shaking their heads indignantly, which secretly pleased him.

"Lots of them!" he said. "If I told you their names, I wouldn't be much of a man. Some had me beat my gong to find their lost kids, then when I found the kids, they refused to pay!"

"Would it have been okay not to pay if you hadn't found the kids?" someone asked.

"Hell no! If Han Qinzai beats his gong, he's got money coming." Now, although he was a small man, owing to a lifetime of shouting as he beat the gong, once he got excited his every word became a virtual shout; but the louder he shouted, the hoarser he grew and the less clearly people understood him. As he talked on, the men unconsciously began to move closer until they were all gathered around him.

Scabby Head, in sympathy with Han Qinzai, said, "That's how it should be. Whoever heard of a matchmaker who was expected to guarantee a bunch of kids in the deal?"

"If everyone was as good as you fellows, we'd never have to talk about conscience," Han Qinzai said. "There's nothing false about what the ancients said. 'There are two men of conscience: he who has died, and he who hasn't been born.'"

The smiles Han Qinzai had anticipated appeared on the faces of all the men present; not only were they interested in what he was saying, they were also gaining respect for him.

"Old Han Qinzai here is no fool. If beating a gong was such a good life, do you think I'd just hand my rice bowl over to someone else?"

They smiled and nodded their heads.

Han Qinzai was always saying "Han Qinzai here, this, that, and the other," and he'd thrust out his chest or tug on his sleeve—each sentence was accompanied by some sort of action. Scabby Head and the others, feeling that he was something special, were filled with envy.

Han Qinzai then turned the conversation around: "But when all is said and done, what you fellows have here is the good life."

"Good?" Scabby Head, who was leaning up against the kadang tree, straightened up and shouted, "Good like hell! Good, you say?"

The others all laughed.

Just as Han Qinzai was about to say something, he was cut off by one of the other men: "If it stays like it has the past few days, we'll all die of starvation!" It had been several days since anyone had visited the shop across the way to buy a coffin.

"It's still too early to be talking about any of us dying!" Han Qinzai stressed the word "us." "What are you fretting about? We haven't come to the end of the line. There's no need to worry. Sooner or later someone's bound to die—if not today, then tomorrow. Who knows, maybe the day after tomorrow a bunch of people will come to buy coffins all at once!" He felt that this was just the right thing to say.

"God, no, not all at the same time! One a day is perfect." This was Turtle's opinion.

"Is that what you really think?" Know-It-All asked critically. "One a day? I don't know how you'd handle it all. Each one is good for two or three days, so one every two or three days is just about right. That way, as soon as we finish up with one, we can move right on to another..."

Before he had a chance to finish, Fire Baby piped up angrily, "Don't be stupid! Do you think you're King Yama of Hell or something?"

Know-It-All was stunned by the severity of Fire Baby's tone of voice. Taking the roar of laughter from the men as approval, Fire Baby proudly hammered his point home: "Don't you interfere with the business of King Yama. You're talking like a fucking idiot!"

Blockhead, who had been sitting there listening to the conversation, grinning from ear to ear and looking like the potbellied Maitreya Buddha, suddenly stood up excitedly and began to babble like a child: "Go ahead and have everybody drop dead! Go ahead and have everybody drop dead!"

His outburst drew curses from the others:

"Fuck you, Blockhead!" one shouted.

"You drop dead yourself!" said another.

"Children should be seen and not heard, Blockhead!" shouted yet another.

But Blockhead had thoughts only for his own laughter, and for the cigarette butts in the hands of his cronies. He reached down and picked up the butt Han Qinzai had just discarded. These men always pinched the tips of their cigarettes lightly between their fingers. They had smoked this way so long that the nicotine stains on their fingers had turned from yellow to a dark brown. And even though the nearness of the lit ends burned their fingers, they continued to smoke them unhurriedly, as if there were absolutely nothing to be concerned about. It was indeed a rarity for this group of men (Han Qinzai included) to smoke cigarettes of Long Life quality. The mildness and aromatic smell of the smoke coupled with the feelings of grandeur he was experiencing had Han Qinzai in their spell. But then the image of five or six hands stretching out to him ruined the moment, and all he could do was swallow hard a couple of times.

The only effect of everyone's curses on Blockhead was a continuous peal of idiotic giggling emanating from his nostrils, since his mouth remained closed the whole time. It was a weird snorting sound. The others' response was a mixture of hilarity and anger. Fire Baby ran over and pulled Blockhead's whiskers, but the idiotic giggling continued, and even when his whiskers were pulled hard enough to hurt, Blockhead would only say dispiritedly, "Don't do that! Don't!"

Scabby Head took a final puff on his cigarette and flipped the butt away. Blockhead, paying no attention to Fire Baby, casually edged his fat body over to the spot, but Fire Baby jumped in ahead of him and stepped on the butt. Blockhead merely tried to shove Fire Baby out of the way, his action more symbolic than substantial.

"If you promise to wash your ass nice and clean tonight, Fire Baby'll move his foot," Scabby Head said.

Blockhead, still in control of his temper, continued shoving Fire Baby and saying, "Don't say that! Don't! Scabby Head, don't say that!"

"Call me 'Daddy.' If you'll call me 'Daddy,' I'll move my foot."

"Don't do that! Daddy, don't."

Hearing him call Fire Baby "Daddy," the others squealed with laughter. Just then the sounds of chopping and sawing from the coffin shop stopped, and this cessation of activity across the street brought the merriment of the group of men under the kadang tree to a halt; Han Qinzai's laughter, alone, hung in the air for an instant as the other men turned their gazes to the coffin shop. What they saw was three pairs of surprise-filled eyes staring back at them. Blockhead's childlike speech and intolerable giggling broke the silence of this moment. Amid the ensuing laughter the voice of the owner of the coffin shop was still discernible: "Drop dead, you fucking Blockhead!"

The few men who had been sleeping soundly through all this

were rudely awakened by the extraordinarily raucous laughter.

Han Qinzai's chatter was well received by one and all. In fact, Scabby Head told him whenever he had nothing to do to come over and pass the time with them. Han Qinzai was already aware that Scabby Head was the leader of the group, so he carried a secret happiness with him on the road home. The knowledge that he too would someday have his spot under the kadang tree wiped his mind clean of worries and anger over his loss of a livelihood, and even his concern over his outstanding debts. He nonchalantly turned his steps toward the road on which the tobacco and wine shop whose owner pressed him the hardest to clear his bill was located. He was making mental calculations: if he returned tomorrow and his luck was good, a customer might show up at the coffin shop and he could take part in the funeral procession; with food to eat and a handout as well, he would be in seventh heaven! The more he thought about tomorrow, the greater the possibility loomed. It had been a long time since anyone had bought a coffin, a situation that could not last much longer. His only fear had been that a coffin might have been sold the day before he showed up, which would have meant a delay of several days for him.

So engrossed in his thoughts was he that the sudden appearance of the Temple of Matsu, the Goddess of the Sea, brought him rudely back to his senses—he had inadvertently walked right up next to Longevity General Store. He was about to turn on his heel and get out of there when someone inside the store spotted him. The jig was up. He had a sinking feeling. Quickening his pace, he turned his face away from the store, steeled himself, and walked on. But it was too late. He distinctly heard someone behind him call out "Han Qinzai," although he ignored the shout and kept walking, hoping that the other man would think it was a case of mistaken identity. But the fellow was not fooled. He not only continued to shout Han Qinzai's name but also ran after him. Grabbing him by the shoulder, he pulled Han Qinzai to a halt and cursed him angrily: "Fuck you and all your ancestors! Come on, run—let's see you run away now. I'll bet you can't sprout wings and fly off."

Han Qinzai had been jerked to a stop so abruptly he nearly tumbled to the ground.

"I wasn't running away," he said innocently. "I wasn't."

"You weren't running away? If you weren't running away, why didn't you stop when I called you?"

"I didn't hear you call me."

"You didn't hear me! Ha! Are your ears plugged up with shit? Huh?" With each sentence, Longevity gave Han Qinzai's shoulders two or three rough shakes, so that his frail body rocked back and forth in the man's hands as though he were suspended in air. "You want me to clean them out with the manure spade? Huh? What do you say?"

"Brother Longevity, let me go! Please, I beg you." Han Qinzai cast embarrassed looks around him at the crowd that was gathering, then said to Longevity in a soft voice, "Let me keep a little face in front of all these people, okay? Please let me go."

"Hai! A man like you worrying about *face*! Did you all hear that?" Longevity smugly turned toward the crowd and, with a laugh, said in a loud voice, "This is what's called 'putting face before life itself!'"

Han Qinzai, with his frail body, was like a mouse caught in the grasp of a cat, tossed around so violently that onlookers were concerned that his innards might get all jumbled up. Sensing that the people gathering to watch all this commotion had formed a huge crowd that covered the handcar turntable, Han Qinzai was so embarrassed he felt like crawling into a hole and hiding. He'd always felt he had some status in this town, but now that was gone. On top of that, what remained of his will to implore for the return of even a little dignity had crumbled. His spirits were paralyzed, his most instinctive behavior consciously repressed; if it was necessary to lose face, all he had to say was, "So what? If I'm broke, I'm broke! My flesh has a salty taste, so what can you do about it?" But he figured he'd beg one more time, and if that didn't work, he'd go ahead and blurt it out and let that be the end of it.

"Brother Longevity, I'm not your senior, though I am older than you. Let me go, please. If I had the money, I'd pay you," he said softly, a weak smile on his face.

"If you had the money?" Longevity laughed as though he were on the verge of hysteria. "If you had the money, then everyone in the world would be rich!"

Han Qinzai could stand it no longer; he was about to wrench himself free of Longevity's grasp and shout out savagely, "My flesh has a salty taste, so what can you do about it?" when he heard someone in the crowd say, "That's Han Qinzai, the gong beater." Suddenly he grew weak, sensing that if he were to take a truculent attitude, this thing called "Han Qinzai" would surely be beaten to a pulp.

"Uncle Longevity," he said, "have a little compassion. Until I pay back the money I owe you, let all my luck be bad. Okay? Worthy Uncle Longevity…" He was about to ask Longevity once more to let him go, but he guessed that the more he pleaded to be released, the more Longevity would be inclined to hold fast, so he made up his mind not to ask again. He merely repeated himself: "Worthy Uncle Longevity…"

All this evoked peals of laughter from the crowd of onlookers. And finally, Longevity, seeing no alternative, released his grasp.

"If you don't pay me next time, I'm not going to let you off so easily! Next time I'll rip the clothes right off your back."

Amid the laughter from the crowd, someone said, "Longevity is quite the fellow—look how big a grandson he's got!"

"My luck isn't that bad!" Longevity commented in obvious high spirits.

Standing off to the side, feeling very embarrassed and at a loss as to what to do with himself, Han Qinzai merely examined his wrinkled clothes and tried to smooth them out with his hand. He didn't hear a word of the clamor coming from the crowd. Now that the affair was closed, he didn't even have the good sense to leave the scene.

Longevity returned to his store; the crowd of curious spectators surrounded Han Qinzai as he stood there with a vacant stare on his face. Then the whole scene began to resemble a strange type of fruit: the people were the skin, which at this moment began to peel itself off, layer by layer, until all that remained was the pit—Han Qinzai—cast aside there at the turntable. He was still absent-mindedly smoothing a wrinkled spot on his clothing with his hand. Chagrin filled his heart. *I shouldn't have let him do that to me! I should've told him right off the bat, "My flesh has a salty taste, so what are you going to do about it?" Now that he's let me go, I can't look anyone in the face. I really shouldn't have called him "worthy uncle" or "worthy elder brother"! Worthy, ha!* His feelings of regret increased. He knew that no one was watching him any longer, but he simply could not raise his head, which seemed to weigh a ton.

Off in the distance some people were pushing a handcar toward him. They were on their way here to the turntable to get on the track heading toward the ocean. The driver was shouting. Finally coming to his senses, Han Qinzai left in a hurry. As cautiously and alertly as a mouse, he made his way back to the air-raid shelter in the park.

The moment he entered he threw himself noisily onto the bed, and before he knew it, tears were coursing down his face. He began to sniffle and was soon crying. Never before, in the twenty or thirty years of his adult life, had he shed a single tear. After somewhat regaining his composure, he sat up, cursing over and over in a heavy voice, "Fuck your old lady, fuck your old lady...." After a while he reached over to get the rag that was draped over the head of his bed, with which he wiped his tear-streaked face. Sensing a warmth and soreness on his right cheek, he reached up to touch it and discovered that he had two scratches. He paced back and forth in the air-raid shelter until he happened to notice his gong lying beneath the bed. He took it out and examined it.

"All right!" he said resolutely. "If I ever get another chance to go out on the streets and beat this gong again, I'm definitely going to start saving some money."

IT'S ALL RIGHT TO WATCH PEOPLE DRINK TONICS, BUT DON'T WATCH DOGS FIGHT OVER A BONE

By the following day, Han Qinzai had put together a story of how he'd received the scratches on his right cheek. As soon as he saw the men under the kadang tree he said, "There's truth to the saying that lightning only strikes good men." He rubbed his cheek. "After I left here yesterday, just as I was passing the

Cultivation Pharmacy, I picked up some peanuts from the ground to feed to the two monkeys, and who'd have guessed that when I raised my head one of them would grab hold and scratch my face? I hope the damned beast dies an early death!"

"That's for sure! The two monkeys at the Cultivation Pharmacy are famous for their pranks. Not long ago a woman was walking past there when the same thing happened to her—one of them grabbed hold of her head and wouldn't let go," Fire Baby said.

"What happened to her afterward?" Know-It-All asked, his interest piqued.

"You're the horniest guy around. You wake up as soon as anyone mentions a woman," Fire Baby said, his mouth cracked in a wide grin, as he led the others in a round of laughter.

Know-It-All, apparently intimidated by Fire Baby, replied, "Then… then why did you bring it up?"

"You want to know, do you?" Fire Baby said. "Well, since you want to know, I'm going to tell you." He puffed himself up, and even his words had a ring of affectation. "Afterward, afterward, uh, the woman got married and had some kids… ha ha!"

Han Qinzai squatted on his haunches, and when the laughter had just about died out, he said, rubbing his scratched face, "Damn him, I hope the hand that scratched me rots off!" He was thinking about Longevity, but what he said was, "A pharmacy ought to gain a reputation by selling quality medicines, not by having its monkeys scratch people."

"That's right," said Fire Baby, who was now sitting beside Han Qinzai. "Got any of those Long Life cigarettes left over from yesterday?" There was a marked contrast in the tone of the two separate utterances. He thrust his neck out, sort of like a throat specialist looking down the throat of a patient. His eyes were glued to Han Qinzai's shirt pocket.

Han Qinzai patted the pocket and, with a wry smile, said he didn't.

"Does a chicken with a crooked beak get any of the good feed?" the man named Mongrel, who was sitting beneath another kadang tree, spat out.

"What's that got to do with you?" Fire Baby leaped to his feet. "What are you thinking, you damned ingrate?"

"What's it to you? You looking for trouble?"

Mongrel's response was strong; he got to his feet and said with a cunning sneer, "Aha! So you've finally found a pretext."

"Come over a little closer if you've got the guts."

This was said so loudly that the speaker seemed about to explode.

Laughing lightheartedly but with anger in his eyes, Mongrel took a few steps forward, his glare never leaving the other man's face.

"So, are you going to stand there and let me beat the shit out of you, or are you going to mix it up? You'll treat me for free or you'll have it delivered to my door."

Fire Baby's hands were already clenched into fists; his arms hung stiffly at his sides; he took two or three steps forward to show he wasn't backing down.

Only a single pace now separated the two men. Seeing this state of affairs, Han Qinzai began to tremble. He was hoping someone would step in and break it up, but when he looked back at the others, he discovered that they were all sitting or reclining on the ground, so hot they looked a bit dopey. Their eyes were glued to the two men squaring off, and they were enjoying the prospect of a fight that loomed before them. It looked like it was going to start any second now.

"Isn't anyone going to step in?" Han Qinzai asked anxiously, his eyes sweeping their faces. "Hurry, somebody do something!" As he made his plea he walked up close to the two men.

"Why trouble yourself, Han Qinzai? When the weather's as hot as it is today, it takes too much energy to break up a fight," someone said.

Fire Baby and Mongrel were already shoving each other. Their anger was no longer as strong as when the incident had begun, and when they heard Han Qinzai coming to make peace between them, saying "Come... come on, listen to me now," they decided to take advantage of these peacemaking attempts to gain a moral victory before the fight was called off. There wasn't going to be any fight now anyway, they thought, so their pushing and shoving grew more heated, to the point that they were both grunting. Han Qinzai, who had had thoughts of stepping in to break things up, moved off to the side when he saw how hard they were shoving. His mediations were limited to the vocal, not the physical variety: "Ai! Ai! Don't fight, don't fight. Someone hurry up and pull them apart!"

"Don't pay any attention to them, Han Qinzai. Don't spoil their fun," Scabby Head shouted.

Han Qinzai just stood there, not knowing what to do.

Both Mongrel and Fire Baby were scrawny men, so everywhere you looked they were small, except for their joints—knees, elbows, chins, and cheeks—all of which jutted out almost frighteningly. This was particularly true with their shoulders: a loose layer of skin covered sharply jutting shoulder bones, and as they bumped each other, not only did they make sounds like stones banging under water, but they felt sharp pains reaching down to the marrow. It was too late to lessen the force of the bumps—having mounted the tiger, it was hard to climb down. Matters having reached this stage, the two could only bump each other even harder to determine who would be the victor, thereby bringing this standoff to its conclusion. Their thoughts were identical. They bumped each other once more, then stepped back before going at it again; this time they both lowered their center of gravity and were almost crouching as they faced each other—this would really do the trick. The stinging pain from the last encounter was most severe in Mongrel's shoulder, but he couldn't stop now. Just as they lurched at each other this time, Mongrel twisted his body slightly and Fire Baby brushed past him, looking like a catapulted missile as he crashed headlong to the ground, where a kadang tree stopped him.

Everyone burst out laughing as they saw him sprawled there. "That's a mighty force," one of them said. "Look at all the leaves he's knocked down!" Fire Baby was fiery mad. He turned around, fists waving menacingly in the air, and without a thought for how things would turn out, rushed forward like a madman. Han Qinzai was more frightened than ever, but before the charging Fire Baby could get to where they were standing, Han Qinzai placed himself in front of Mongrel, spread out his hands, and shouted, "For God's sake, don't! For God's sake, don't! For God's sake..." The wild anger of Fire Baby had produced a similar reaction of anger in Mongrel. Ignoring Han Qinzai's attempt to place himself as an obstacle between the two of them, Mongrel tried to push him out of the way, but it was too late—Fire Baby was upon them. With Han Qinzai standing between the combatants, they swung their fists and the battle was on. Han Qinzai couldn't get out of the way. When one of them kicked, the other kneed; when one of them clawed, the other ripped and tore, until they all tumbled to the ground in a pile.

Neither Mongrel nor Fire Baby could get the upper hand, but as they were rolling on the ground in a stalemate, they both suddenly felt comfortably rested. They were still grappling with each other, but a mutual agreement to stop the fisticuffs had been silently reached, and neither wanted to strike the next blow. They puffed and panted as sweat poured down their faces; then, as they suddenly felt how ridiculously funny it all was, their mouths parted as the laughter welling up inside them burst forth.

The person who got the worst of it all was Han Qinzai. With the two men on top, pinning him to the ground, he lay there covering up his head, not daring to move. His eyes shut tightly, he just kept mumbling over and over, "For God's sake, don't! For God's sake, don't!"

"That's enough, now, that's enough!" Scabby Head said as he lazily got to his feet. "You've nearly squashed poor Han Qinzai to death!"

Mongrel and Fire Baby reacted as if they'd been waiting for someone to call them to a halt, for as soon as they heard Scabby Head's shouts, they let go of each other and stood up. When they saw the shape Han Qinzai was in, they started to laugh.

"Ram it up your…! Go ahead and fight! Show me how you can fight! Old Scabby Head here will treat you both to some fried noodles if you're still able to slug it out!" Scabby Head lectured them with the airs of a leader.

Han Qinzai still lay on his side, mumbling over and over, "For God's sake, don't!" unaware that he should be getting up off the ground.

"You've squashed his soul right out of his body," Scabby Head said, walking over to take a look.

The smiles disappeared from Mongrel's and Fire Baby's faces. They just stood there dumbly looking on while the others crowded around to watch Scabby Head examining Han Qinzai.

"The poor guy," Scabby Head said. "Does anyone know how to locate his revival tendon?"

No answer. The men just stared dumbly into each other's faces, their eyes opened wider than usual.

Scabby Head lifted up Han Qinzai's black shirt and felt around under his armpits; he stopped suddenly, as though he had found something, then pinched down so hard that even his own mouth twisted sharply. Han Qinzai let out a yelp, which instilled Scabby Head with confidence. "So that's all there is to locating the revival tendon!" He pinched again, hard, which elicited a "What the fuck!" from Han Qinzai. This quickly put everyone at ease, and their eyes returned to normal size. Blockhead was the first to break the stifling atmosphere the incident had produced with his unbearable giggles. Know-It-All, childishly hopping around like a sparrow, dashed over behind Blockhead, reached around him, and squeezed his fat, slightly sagging breasts. Life had returned to this tiny section of the world.

Han Qinzai's every movement, from sitting up to getting to his feet to starting to talk, was carefully scrutinized. All this made him feel as though he were invested with some special privileges. The other men watched him with smiling eyes (no, in One-Eye's case you would have to say smiling eye—his left one—for his right eye never opened and, in fact, was recessed deeply in its socket), waiting to see what he would do.

Han Qinzai felt and rubbed himself all over, squealing with pain and filling the air with four-letter words as he did so. More rubbing and feeling, until there was no place he had missed. During his self-examination, the other men received every shout and every curse with sympathy and good-natured laughs, and their sympathy was no less generous just because there was a little exaggeration on his part. As a result, he did not feel too strongly that he had been abused. He did sense, however, that he must take advantage of the moment, now that they were all on his side. Brushing the dust off his clothing, he was of a mind to blow his stack and show them that he was no one to fool with, but after some reasoned reflection, he said fatalistically:

"'It's all right to watch people drink tonics, but don't watch dogs fight over a bone.'" He smiled. "Hai! The ancients sure knew what was what. We can follow their lead. Me, I'm all muddle-headed. Ai! A real muddle head."

"I think you ought to take some medicine in case you have any internal injuries," Fire Baby said. "I'll recommend some herb medicine for you." He cocked his head. "Horsewhip grass is the best. After it's ground into a pulp, if you're a drinking man, you can add some wine; if not, take it with some brown sugar. It's guaranteed. I've cured a lot of people with it."

"Mixing up some horsewhip grass is easy. You can find all you want at Graveyard Harbor."

Han Qinzai turned to look at the person who was making suggestions for his well-being.

"There's something else that's not bad," Scabby Head said. "Banyan bristles pounded into a pulpy liquid and drunk straight is good for internal injuries. It doesn't taste as bad as horsewhip grass and there's no smell."

"If you're going to take something, do it now."

"Right, right," Han Qinzai said.

THE GONG

"It's only fair to have Mongrel and Fire Baby go pick the grass."

"That's all right, I'll get it myself. All they need to do is buy the wine."

"Sure, sure, that's fair enough."

Several of the men voiced their agreement.

"But I don't have any money now," Mongrel complained, scratching his head. "We haven't had a funeral banquet for a long time."

It *had* been a long time, probably a week since they'd last seen a customer at the coffin shop. But it seemed to take Mongrel's comment to force home the seriousness of their dilemma. The sweltering heat had their nerves on edge. Anxieties flooded their minds, and Han Qinzai's injuries quickly faded into insignificance.

"We're not heartless, but it's really been a long time since anyone died."

"What are you so worried about? There's a meal coming right around the corner," Han Qinzai said.

"Who?" Their eyes lit up.

"Scholar Yang. It's sure to be lavish."

"Balls! They were making noises about him breathing his last years ago, and they're still making those noises today."

"That old fart is holding on for dear life," Fire Baby said.

"Eleven of his twelve souls are already gone, and the last one won't let go of the threshold—you'd hold on for dear life too!"

"Ai! He ought to give it up. The old guy isn't very smart—by hanging on like this he's lost the filial respect of the younger ones. What good does that do anybody?"

Han Qinzai's mention of Scholar Yang led to a lengthy discussion, but nothing came of it, and with the weather as hot as it was, the longer the discussion lasted the less spirited it grew.

The clamor of the moment before and their light mood gradually began to settle earthward like dust. One by one they took up their favorite positions and lapsed into a dull-witted immobility. Han Qinzai was not accustomed to this sort of reticence. After racking his brain for a few moments, he came up with a subject for conversation. Tossing a pebble over Scabby Head's way, he said:

"Hey Scabby Head, people say that if there's no business at the coffin shop, all you have to do is strike a coffin three times with a broom, and the next day someone will come over to buy a coffin. Do you believe that?"

"I've heard that, but I've never tried it myself."

"I wonder if the owner of the coffin shop knows about it."

"Everyone knows. If it worked, he wouldn't just let his business peter out like this."

"Maybe he's never tried it," Han Qinzai said, holding out a ray of hope. "What do you say?"

The others didn't want to be left out of this discussion, and although they didn't actually say anything, they had at least snapped out of their gloomy mood.

"Let's give it a try," Han Qinzai said excitedly. "Who's going to do it?"

"Any one of us, me included."

"Well, speak up."

The others shrank back, their smiles showing that they wanted to be excluded. They cast glances back and forth.

"Look," Han Qinzai whispered, "the coffin shop owner and his two apprentices have knocked off for lunch. And look over there, to the left: there's a broom standing against the wall. If we're going to do it, now's our chance."

"Who's going?"

"Let's draw straws," Mongrel offered.

"Draw straws! They'll be back outside before you've got the straws cut and drawn." Han Qinzai wanted badly to try it himself. This was just what the doctor ordered to get on their good side.

"So what'll we do?" Mongrel was getting a little anxious. So was Han Qinzai. He was afraid that if he allowed Mongrel to be the first to volunteer, he'd lose a ready-made opportunity to distinguish himself. Observing the expression on Mongrel's face and afraid that he was about to open his mouth to speak up, Han Qinzai blurted out, "I'll go!" He looked at the others. "By the time you guys get around to doing anything, you've missed your chance!"

As the others looked at Han Qinzai, the volunteer, respect was written all over their faces, which redoubled his boldness. Taking a deep breath, he made ready to dash across the street.

"Keep an eye on the road for me. If anyone comes, give a yell." With that, he ran across. Looking back over his shoulder, he saw all the men under the kadang tree holding their breath and watching his every move in motionless silence; they were so still they seemed about to pop.

Han Qinzai walked over beneath the eaves of the building, then looked up and down the street before darting on ahead. He picked up the broom, carried it over to the nearest coffin, rapped on it three times—*bang, bang, bang*—then scurried back across the street, still holding on to the broom.

The men had started to roar the moment they saw him pick up the broom, and the sight of him rushing back, broom in hand, had them holding their sides with laughter.

"You guys are real losers. I just risked my life for you!"

They were by now laughing uncontrollably.

"You bunch of ignorant pigs!" He was waving the broom in the air as a symbol of his contribution.

Scabby Head was holding his sides, laughing at the sight of Han Qinzai with the broom in his hand.

"Aiya! Mother! The... the broom... oh, it's killing me!"

Everyone was aware of the humor of the situation, and the waves of laughter reached the ears of the two apprentices at the coffin shop, who emerged to see what was going on, their rice bowls still in their hands.

"Hey, Han Qinzai, your broom..." someone said softly.

By this time the laughter had stopped completely as the men glanced back and forth across the street, then at Han Qinzai. He had been completely in the dark until the word "broom" was mentioned. When he came to his senses and saw what was happening, he froze on the spot.

"Hide it—hurry, they're looking at you."

As he jerked his head around to look across the street, someone came up and yanked the broom out of his hand, threw it to the ground, and sat on it with one of the other men.

The two apprentices continued to shove rice into their mouths as they watched the activity on the opposite side of the street. But seeing that nothing much was going on, they went back inside. Han Qinzai breathed a sigh of relief, then began to sense the humor in the situation.

"How could I have carried the broom back with me?" he said. "What a lunkhead I am."

"I think you were giddy."

"Where's the broom? I'll take it back over."

"Since nothing's happened, just forget it. We'll toss it away later."

"Ai! How... how can we do that?"

"Don't worry about it," Scabby Head said. "Tomorrow we'll see if your plan's worked."

"Well, I... I've already done my part."

Although no one said anything in response, Han Qinzai could tell from their smiling faces that they had accepted him and that he was covered with glory.

But then, just as he was receiving their accolades, his heart was troubled by a nagging anxiety. He began to regret what he had just done, for if someone were actually to come to buy a coffin on the following day, wouldn't he, Han Qinzai, be responsible for the person's death? *I've already lived half a lifetime, and although I might not be considered a particularly "good" man, I've never been a particularly "bad" one either—and certainly not one to cause someone's death. I can only hope and pray that the whole experiment falls through.* He sat down on the ground with his eyes closed, his back resting against the kadang tree, as he contemplated his situation.

He was completely oblivious to the words of praise, meaningful or casual, with which the group of men were rewarding him, and to their recounting of the rollicksome effects his daring venture had produced. He didn't even feel like bothering with them; he was too wrapped up in the feeling that he had sunk into a deep, dark abyss. He just sat there and thought. A stream of fond memories of events from his past, even those of little consequence, filled his mind. He no longer had to feel badly about his loss of income, but he did lament with considerable pain the cessation of the jobs he had been given, jobs that had filled him with a sense of esteem rather than subjecting him to ridicule.

* * *

A mother stood at the entrance to the air-raid shelter calling out in mournful tones, "Gong beater! Gong beater!" Then a pause. "Is the gong beater here?"

"Yeah! Here I am!" Han Qinzai awoke from his nap and jumped to his feet.

"Please come outside."

"I'm coming! I'm coming!"

As he stepped through the shelter entrance he was temporarily blinded by the bright sunlight. The woman began talking to him before he could even make out who she was.

"My child, Axiong, is lost." After saying the words "my child," the woman choked up and her speech was barely intelligible.

Han Qinzai knew exactly what this young mother was feeling. He consoled her: "I know, I know. Your child is lost, isn't he?" The sobbing woman nodded.

"Don't worry, just tell me slowly how big he is, how I can recognize him, what he's wearing, and where you think he might be. When did you notice he was missing? That should do it."

"He… he…" The woman was trying hard to speak, but all she could do was sob.

"That's all right, don't worry. There isn't a lost child anywhere I can't find. You go ask around and see if I'm not telling the truth. And I can find yours just as easily."

The young mother was greatly reassured. "His name is Axiong," she said. "He has big eyes, and he's very cute. We say he's three, but he's actually only two." She stopped and thought a moment, and as she did, her mournful appearance suddenly gave way to a look of sheer love. "I took him with me to buy a piece of material to cut up and make some diaper pants for him. While I was looking over the material in the shop, he was fussing to get down and play, so I told him not to go into the street—he even made a sound that he understood me." The mournful look reappeared.

Han Qinzai took advantage of the break in her narration to ask some questions, until he finally got all the information he needed.

"Okay, that's all I need to know. You go back and look for him. Your best bet is to go down to the big drainage ditch and look around there. I'll start with the gong right away, and everything will be fine."

He turned on his heel and picked up his gong, then fell in behind the young mother and started beating it.

> *Bong! Bong! Bong!*
> *The gong beater's coming your way—*
> *Listen everyone, here's what I have to say—*
> *A child, his name is Axiong—*
> *Three years old, but really only two—*
> *His eyes big as flower buds, cute as a bug's ear;*
> *Barefoot, black open-crotch pants, a white shirt—*
> *Anyone seeing him take him to the police station right away—*
> *Or to the quilt shop beside the Temple of the Patriarch—*
> *Axiong's mother is on pins and needles—*
> *Bong! Bong! Bong!*

No one in the entire town escaped the sound of Han Qinzai's gong that afternoon. Around dusk, the mother came running up the street, Axiong cradled in her arms, to catch up with Han Qinzai. She expressed her gratitude over and over, then thrust a red envelope into his hand. There hadn't been much money in it, but as he thought back on it now, it had impressed him as a rich recompense.

* * *

Ai! I hope and pray I haven't killed anyone, and I wish I hadn't done that stupid thing. The feeling that his heart was bobbing around in a deep, dark abyss would not go away.

It was obvious to the others that the expression on Han Qinzai's face was vastly different than the heroic look of a moment before.

"Han Qinzai, what's wrong?"

He heard them but did not feel like answering.

"He probably really was injured," Scabby Head said, his eyes scanning the faces of Mongrel and Fire Baby.

"I, I'll go get some horsewhip grass for you, okay?" Fire Baby volunteered apologetically.

A smile appeared on Han Qinzai's face and his eyes flashed open. The pale faces of the concerned men who had gathered around him lit up immediately. He had obviously gained acceptance into the group, just as he had planned, except that it had happened more quickly than he'd anticipated. He was not surprised; he just felt a bit degenerate. It was this indefinable sense of degeneracy that by rights should have alarmed him, for it was the one thing he had not counted on. And this unexpected development was fearful enough to alarm him as it began to crush down on him with deadening force. This was the first time Han Qinzai had come face to face with the specter of degeneracy. "It's nothing, just a nagging old problem. I'll be all right after I've rested a moment."

"But don't take it lightly. You don't want something like this to turn into a chronic injury. That'd be a real problem."

He sensed that he was too easily deceived. The scorn in which he had so recently held these men had been completely and immediately obliterated by a few kind words.

"I won't. I'll go get some horsewhip grass in just a moment." There were no pains anywhere on his body; casually stroking his chest, he said, "I don't think there's anything wrong."

Everyone smiled weakly.

COCKCROW SIGNALS A HAPPY EVENT

He experienced a feeling of lightheadedness as soon as he got up from under the kadang tree, and he never could have gotten to his feet at all if he hadn't been able to close his eyes and hold on to the tree trunk. He sat down on the cement block at the entrance to the air-raid shelter, his face buried in his hands. He figured it was probably because of his yam diet; otherwise... *Oh-oh! Here it comes again.* Brightness suddenly replaced the haziness in his brain; it gradually turned yellow, then green, then red; then the encircling haziness returned. At this instant, his entire being seemed to be a mere shell that had had something drained from it. Fortunately, he was sitting down at the moment, or he would surely have collapsed. He readied himself for the next attack, which he knew would surely come. He continued to hold his head in his hands, and his body was tense and coiled—even his toes were curled inward. These dizzy spells had troubled him a great deal of late; sometimes he was able to bring one under control through sheer willpower alone, while at other times the force of his will had the effect of increasing their severity. He had gradually learned to cope with these two situations by trial and error: when the oncoming spell was controllable, he would increase the force of his willpower very gradually; when control was out of the question, he would gradually slacken it, for if he were to let the dizzy spell take complete hold of him with a rush, he would immediately begin retching or, even worse, crumple to the ground like a man losing a judo match. After a long while, and then an even longer while, before the second attack hit him, his muscles began to relax and loosen like lumps of kneaded dough. Once they were relaxed, the spell had passed, but still he raised his head gingerly, the chill sweeping over his body making him realize that he was sweating. The scene before him was too bright, like an overexposed photograph. He propped himself up on the cement, then steadied himself with the aid of the damp wall and placed his hand on his bed. A current of warmth ran up along his arm all the way to his heart. Once he lay down in bed this current of warmth flowed out of his body.

An oppressive darkness surrounded him, which, by comparison, made him fade into infinite insignificance. He was powerless to move. It was as if he'd been placed there expressly to lie on his side and sleep facing the wall. He was totally alert. Amid the darkness, beads of water on the damp wall slowly came into view, reflecting light seeping in through the entrance as they slithered down the wall. Han Qinzai, who had no concept of time, suddenly felt very keenly time's swift passage. *Tomorrow will be here soon. Have I killed anyone? I'll know tomorrow.* He was deeply superstitious and had gone through life comforted by a conviction that the gods were protecting him. Wasn't it true, he thought, that on the day before the birthday of every temple god, it was he who beat his gong to inform the town faithful? And on each of the festive temple processions or excursions of the gods, it was he who led the way, waving his red-festooned mallet and beating his gong. *Shit, now I don't even have this to fall back on.* He was seeing a tradition crumble right before his eyes, as though it were a gigantic statue crashing to the ground. And since it was crumbling through his fingers, the guilt, he felt, was his. Yet all he could do was curse the cause—which was not at all clear to him. "Shit!"

Much of the light from the entrance had faded, so the drops of water on the damp wall were no longer visible. Mosquitoes buzzed around his ears, sounding like the fading resonance of a struck gong—as though the gong that lay beneath his bed and served as a container for odds and ends were making sounds: *bong, bong, bong.* Beneath the scorching sun the gong was reverberating. He wiped his sweat repeatedly with the hand that had held the mallet. He screamed at the top of his voice; the salt from his sweat was stinging his eyes. Golden flashes of light from the surface of the gong were blinding him. He screamed once more at the top of his voice. He still could not hear the sound of his own screams. Sweat continued to ooze from his pores. He tried again: the faces of passersby crushed in on him, huge and threatening, and he ran like a madman, with many people chasing him wordlessly. He could run no farther; holding the gong tightly to his chest, he squatted down on his haunches, exposing his back until it was chilled, but when he turned around, there was nothing. The drops of water on the wall were still not visible. He could hear his heart thumping so that it seemed about to burst through his chest wall.

He wiped the sweat with his clothing as he lay gazing intently at the ventilation opening. Originally a smokestack that had been carried over and buried deep in a mound of earth, this opening now served as the shelter's source of ventilation. Strangely, no matter how hard it rained, the water had never seeped in through it. Sometimes Han Qinzai would use a brick to plug up the opening, but not today.

Through it he could see a circular patch of blue poking through the pitch-blackness above him and moving with his gaze. If he had seen a bright star up there in that patch of blue, he'd have known that the night was still early. But he saw nothing, only the blue that filled the space above him and kept floating past. It did not capture his attention. He rolled over and lay facing the wall, thinking about the coming day. *They're a bunch of disgusting pigs.* He yawned and his eyes watered. He closed his eyes and wiped the moisture away; he didn't feel like opening his eyes anymore. *The fucking pigs!* He could hear Blockhead's inane giggles. *That guy can go to hell!* Know-It-All's grimy, protruding navel—*Whew!* One-Eye's sunken eyelid; the hernia that bumped on the ground whenever Gold Clock squatted down; Scabby Head's pate, which looked like it had been gnawed on by a dog, plus his runny nose and rotting ear lobes. *A bunch of pigs!* He drew his itchy leg up to scratch it. *I never knew what scabies were, but whenever you fall on hard times you run up against just about everything.* He flicked his fingernails, yawned, wiped his watery eyes, made clicking noises with his mouth, and finally swallowed. *I hope and pray I haven't killed him.*

The shelter was hot and stuffy, and by rights he should have been sleeping in the entranceway. But now several bamboo brooms and scoops were piled in front of it. *Damn them!* He had talked to the men who swept up the park about this, telling them to put their equipment inside, for it was only on hot nights that he slept outside. They'd said that if he wasn't going to sleep inside, he should get out, because they were going to put a door and a lock on the shelter. *Who said I wasn't sleeping there? Damn them!* He yawned again. "Go to sleep now." He said this as if he were coaxing a child to sleep. He rolled over; there were still no stars in the patch of blue above him. He listened intently and with total concentration. *Damn it, it's still early for sure.* The only sounds came from the worms, the frogs, and the water in the fountain. A happy thought suddenly struck him: *If it's not the first watch, it must be the second by now, and I haven't heard the crow of a rooster.* The old saying goes: "The first and second watches signal death, the third and fourth signal happy events," and that's right. That thought led him to another: *I haven't killed anyone, I haven't.* He looked up again and searched the patch of blue. Still no stars. *It must be the first watch. Otherwise it's the second, and not a single crowing sound.*

He rolled back over and faced the wall, yawned, squeezed his watery eyes, then noisily licked his lips a couple of times and swallowed. He did not open his eyes again. *Now go to sleep; it'll be light soon.* But he was too agitated to sleep. His escapades involving the desperate search for yams and the debts he'd accumulated were cast out of his mind as though they'd never existed. *I don't have to wait till tomorrow—I know now that I haven't killed anyone! I'm not a bad person, after all.* With happiness filling his heart, he uttered, "Even if someone actually goes over and buys a coffin tomorrow, that doesn't prove it was my doing. Through the first and second watches there wasn't a single rooster's crow." But a nagging doubt persisted even in the midst of this joy. "I *didn't* hear a rooster's crow! I was awake the whole time!" He listened intently once more. He could no longer detect the sounds of worms or frogs, though the sounds of the water fountain and the wind in the trees sent a chill through him. *I'm going to go to sleep.*

If a rooster's going to crow, then let him. He yawned. *It's past the second watch by now.*

Just as he was comforting himself with this thought, from way off in the distance came the faint sounds of a rooster's crow. This threw a scare into him; then he heard an answering crow from nearby. He rolled over to look up through the ventilation opening, where he saw a star woven into the edge of the patch of blue above him. He smiled at the star. The cold rays of light from this predawn star seemed more lustrous than ever. *Here comes another fellow.* He heaved a long sigh. *How can I avoid aging at this rate?* A weak smile, looking like the trail of a meteor, appeared on his face.

In the oppressively dark shelter, the last hint of a thought had disappeared. His even breathing was at one with the darkness and tranquility of the night. This was the most blissful time of day for him: all the fears, self-doubts, remorse, contradictions, and miseries seeped from his heart and melted into the darkness, leaving him to return to his beginnings, to the womb, where he was just like everyone else. He was oblivious of everything.

GOOD NEWS

As dawn broke, Han Qinzai heard the men who swept the park come and pick up their equipment, and he heard them put it back some time later. He was too lazy to get out of his snug bed. If he could just sleep a while longer, he thought, then he wouldn't have to go out so early to wash up and scrounge something to eat. It would have to be yams, anyway. He wasn't at all anxious. *If I can hold off feeding my belly for a while and make it past noon, I'll have saved myself from a couple of meals.* He smiled wryly.

He never anticipated that he wouldn't wake up till way past noon after going back to sleep. He sat groggily on the edge of the bed for a moment, then reached down and fished the Long Life cigarettes out of the gong. Since he had cut each of them in half in order to make them last as long as possible, he still had about a pack left. While he was at it he took a look at the gong. It lay there, resigned to its fate, a receptacle for old nails of various sizes, a big red button he had found, and a ball of twine. The cigarettes were slightly damp and a little harder on the draw than usual. He decided to go over to the kadang tree and see what was up. Taking out two of the half-cigarettes, he put one behind each ear and walked out of the shelter, making some minor repairs to his conical bamboo hat before putting it on.

When the canopy of the kadang tree came into view in the distance, he heard unusually joyful sounds from beneath it. By the time the men came into view, he was surprised to see that they weren't sitting or lying on the ground. All eight or nine of them were standing up discussing something. Just then one of them spotted him. They spun around. "Here he comes! Here he comes!" Han Qinzai was put on his guard and slowed down, being careful to take quiet steps so as not to interfere with his hearing, but taking care also not to show that he was on his guard. He examined the situation carefully. There didn't seem to be any evidence of indignation among the gathered men; in fact, he noticed that one of them was waving to him. It was immediately obvious from the motion of the man's arm that this was a wave of welcome. This put him at ease, and he quickened his pace.

"Hey! Han Qinzai…" Mongrel called out when he was about ten steps away.

"Shh!" Scabby Head warned Mongrel, his back to the coffin shop. He pointed surreptitiously across the street. "Don't let on to them."

Encouraged by the smiles on their faces, Han Qinzai walked in among the men, who immediately crowded around him.

"Han Qinzai," Scabby Head said, "you did it!"

"Fuck him…" It was not an angry curse; quite the contrary, it was said in praise. They had taken this insulting epithet and turned it into a catchall phrase. "It's a good thing you thought of it. Scholar Yang died! Fuck him!" He pounded Han Qinzai on the shoulder.

Han Qinzai slumped the shoulder that was being pounded and rubbed it with an exaggerated motion. "Hey! Are you crazy? Tsk, tsk, tsk." He laughed. *That's all right, let them go ahead and give me the credit, as long as I know the truth—that it wasn't me who killed Scholar Yang. I was awake through the first and second watches, and not a rooster anywhere crowed.* Putting the respect he was being shown to advantage, he commented, "You should have done the same thing a long time ago yourselves, instead of letting him starve to death."

"You're absolutely right."

"Actually, everyone knows you can drum up business by beating on a coffin with a broom, but no one ever thought of doing it."

"Who *would* have thought of doing it? We all figured it was the coffin shop owner's affair."

As always, before he spoke, One-Eye rolled his sunken eye inward; then he blurted out, "Oh yeah! Well, Han Qinzai thought of it!"

"You said it!" Gold Clock waved his hand. "We're a bunch of dumb blockheads."

Everyone laughed at this, as if no one took exception to his comment. As soon as Blockhead heard that everyone there was a blockhead, he resumed his interminable giggling.

They all sat down, drawing their respect for Han Qinzai back within them, and listened attentively to Scabby Head as he handed out work assignments. Actually, there wasn't much difference among the various jobs, except that those who helped in the kitchen made out a little better in the food department.

"Last time," Scabby Head was saying, his memory temporarily failing him, "last time where did we go?"

"That was when Dewang's son-in-law was crushed under the pile of firewood."

"No," Fire Baby corrected him. "There's been another since then."

"Right. It was when Xishui the fish peddler's mother died."

"No, that was even earlier," Mongrel said.

"What do you mean, no? That's when there was all that fish. Blockhead here almost croaked with an eel bone in his throat. I remember very clearly," Fire Baby said.

"You guys love to argue," Mongrel interrupted, spraying the area with saliva. "If I said it's not right, then it's not. You'll drive everybody nuts!"

"All right, that's enough! If you two want to fight it out, go somewhere else and do it." Scabby Head was getting irritated. "Shit, we haven't had a funeral banquet for a few days, and everyone's gone buggy with hunger."

Blockhead stood to the side muttering to himself, "Tailend was crying like a baby, hee hee…."

"Ah, that's right, it was when Tailend's wife over at Westgate died."

"Right! It was when Tailend's wife died." A smile appeared on Scabby Head's face; now the others had all remembered too. "Well! Blockhead's not such a blockhead today!"

Blockhead just giggled, pleased as he could be.

"Who was in the kitchen when Tailend's wife died?" Scabby Head's glance swept past all of them. "Which ones? Whoever it was, speak up."

Still no answer. They all just looked back and forth.

All of a sudden Know-It-All shouted, "Gold Clock, it was you!"

"Me?" He pointed to himself with the airs of one wrongly accused. "Was it me?"

"It sure was, so no funny business." Know-It-All glared at him. "Your mouth was crammed so full of fish-paste balls you couldn't talk. Am I right or wrong?"

"Ah—" he said embarrassedly. "You know I've got a bad temper, so I'm not about to argue with you."

Everyone knew that this was Gold Clock's way of admitting the fact.

"Fuck your ancestors! You and your big balls! So you wanted another turn in the kitchen! Aren't you afraid we'll slice your hernia off and fry it up as a dish of tripe?" Scabby Head shouted.

Gold Clock muttered angrily to himself, "Big balls? I'll give them to you if you want them." His words were so indistinct that not even the men sitting beside him could tell for sure what he was saying.

Han Qinzai sat there listening to their conversation, at the same time pondering the death of Scholar Yang and wondering if there was any link between it and his broom work of the previous day. But however he looked at it, the finger of accusation never pointed to him. He felt like joining the conversation.

"Hey, hold on a minute, all of you. I've got something to say. At the moment I don't have a suitable job, so for the time being I'm throwing in my lot with you. But as soon as I find a job I'll be leaving. Do you all understand? This is only temporary. I might even be leaving tomorrow. Since it's only temporary, it's hard to make plans." He kept stressing the word "temporary."

"As long as you're willing to join up, there's no problem," Scabby Head said.

"We don't have it so bad here."

"Mm! No, I told you—it's just temporary." Han Qinzai shook his head forcefully, like a man who was trying to shake loose something that had stuck to his face.

"He's right! Nobody who's got a decent job would hang around here."

"To tell you the truth, the brothers here are happy to have you along." Fire Baby said what all of them felt. Their smiles were warm and friendly.

"No, no, no, it's temporary, I say. When the time comes for me to leave, I don't want you to accuse me of having no feelings. I've told you it's only temporary." He was feeling very complacent now, for he had given himself a great deal of face.

AT PEACE WITH THE WORLD

As the group of men approached Scholar Yang's tile-roofed mansion, Han Qinzai stayed behind for a moment. *He was going to die anyway I didn't...* he quietly consoled himself, though it was hard to strip away all the fear in his heart. Not really wanting to enter the main hall, he managed to force himself across somehow. At first he had wanted to turn his face away, but he found himself turning to look at Scholar Yang's likeness on the image altar. In the shop of the one and only town artist, a great number of portraits, minus faces, were placed in readiness until needed. This portrait of Scholar Yang had been one of those paintings, to which the artist had now added the man's features. It was hard to say whether or not it looked like him. Perhaps in his younger years, or if he had gotten a bit older, there might have been some resemblance here and there. When Han Qinzai looked into those eyes, which were at peace with the world, he breathed more easily. He was willing to stop and take a closer look. But no matter where he gazed, his eyes always came back to that other pair of eyes, at peace with the world. He brought his hands together and bowed before the portrait. "Scholar Yang, you're the lucky one. Please look after me."

Scabby Head and the others were told that since Scholar Yang's family already had plenty of help, their services wouldn't be needed for very many days. So they sat on their haunches under the eaves waiting for the funeral to begin, at which time they could start out with all their paraphernalia. They were cursing in lowered voices, particularly Mongrel and One-Eye, who had been assigned kitchen duties. Since Scholar Yang's was the most respected family in the entire town and the rites for him should be splendid, they had decided to add one man as a kitchen helper. At the time, Mongrel was in violent opposition, feeling that two was plenty. Everyone knew what he was so nervous about, but the family blocked his arguments. In a burst of anger, he said, "Just another rich person who lived like a damned beggar!"

Han Qinzai didn't want to squat there alongside the others for fear that someone might see him; even though he wasn't sure what they would think, he knew that he'd feel uncomfortable. So he just walked back and forth beside the bier. The local dramatic troupe, the funeral musicians, and the beggars were all waiting nearby. He could even see the town lunatic, Crazy Cai, standing alone by the rubbish heap laughing to herself for no apparent reason. He walked a few steps, then turned his head back to look at her. "What a fucking shame!" In the days when he was beating the gong, this is what he'd said whenever he gave Crazy Cai a fleeting glance.

He walked a little farther off, then took another glance on the sly. She wasn't a bad-looking woman at all: milky white skin, long legs, firm breasts, and nicely rounded buttocks. *What bewitching eyes!* Han Qinzai pretended to be looking elsewhere, then fixed his attention on Crazy Cai. *This summer she's really blossomed, almost overnight, into a young woman. I always knew that, mad as she was, she'd turn out to be a beautiful woman.* His throat was feeling a little dry and he tried to swallow. But there wasn't a drop of saliva in his mouth, and his desire made him uneasy. "Fuck her!" With this brief curse, he walked off as if he were in pain.

Members of the dramatic troupe were tuning their strings and practicing their wind instruments, the funeral musicians were sounding a few tentative notes, and the whole area began to come to life. Han Qinzai walked under the eaves and said to the others, "Looks like it's about time to start out."

"Scholar Yang's own porters are going to carry the coffin out themselves," Scabby Head said, obviously displeased.

It seemed to Han Qinzai that Scabby Head was blaming *him* for having the corpse turn out to be Scholar Yang, as if it were something he never should have done. "What's up, anyway?" He asked forcefully without actually raising his voice. "It's better than nothing, isn't it?"

No one knew what he was talking about. Propped up behind them were colorful banners made of coarse red, blue, and white material. Since there had been five generations of Scholar Yang's family living under one roof, these long cloth banners, slightly more than a foot in width, were fastened to lengths of bamboo that were a bit longer than the width of the banner. They hung in profusion from bamboo poles on which there were still some leaves. The men's appearance as they sat there was strikingly similar to those limp banners.

Han Qinzai squatted down across the street directly opposite the other men, still unwilling to be publicly associated with them. But since the procession was about to begin, he couldn't move off too far, or he might miss the chance to carry one of the banners and share in the handout. He couldn't imagine what had gotten them so steamed up. All they had to do was join the procession, and at the very least they'd get a couple of free meals and some pocket money for their troubles. If they watched their money closely, it would surely be enough to keep them from going hungry for three days or so, until another stiff came along. So what's wrong with that? *Ptui! Just a bunch of pigs.*

One-Eye—the herniated Gold Clock and Mongrel right behind him—walked purposefully over to Han Qinzai and sat down beside him. Han Qinzai felt as if he were on a seesaw, for the moment they sat down, he felt like standing up. He was getting tense. Afraid of causing them a loss of self-respect, he had no recourse but to keep sitting where he was . Know-It-All and Fire Baby came over and joined them.

"A wealthy household like this shouldn't provide such meager offerings for people like us. We depend on these handouts." The sunken eyelid quivered violently. "The death of the renowned Scholar Yang isn't as big a deal as the death of the mother of Xishui from the marketplace," One-Eye said.

"If they're going to carry him out this way, they're going to be criticized by people on the street," Mongrel said, pressing his face up close to Han Qinzai's nose. Han Qinzai didn't move a muscle. "Everyone knew Scholar Yang."

"As I see it, this is the fault of whoever's in charge. We shouldn't be blaming Scholar Yang," Gold Clock paused. "Han Qinzai, how do you feel about it?" After he'd said his piece, he reached down and rubbed himself.

Han Qinzai just smiled, without saying a word.

"This isn't a loss of face only for Scholar Yang's family—people from miles around will be laughing at us folks from Luodong," One-Eye said with growing agitation.

"They're all nuts! Young folks nowadays never consider the consequences of their actions."

"It's the times. As long as they have money in their pockets, they do what they please, and no one can do a thing about it."

"You there, Know-It-All," One-Eye said, spinning around to face him, "you've got it all wrong. Anyone who wants to live in civilized society has to make sure he does things with other people in mind." He turned back to Han Qinzai, his sunken eyelid fluttering. "Han Qinzai, you've got no axe to grind—am I right or not?"

Han Qinzai smiled and looked at One-Eye's single eye, which seemed nearly capable of talking. One-Eye interpreted this smile as one of support, so he really started to talk. As the men debated back and forth, Han Qinzai alone was occupied with his thoughts. He was thinking about putting some money aside and taking care of Crazy Cai properly. Seeing her standing off in the distance, he experienced such a strong desire he couldn't sit still. He felt like laughing but couldn't say why. He picked up snatches of the conversation around him. "You're way off the mark! You haven't got a prayer of ever getting into the matter of society—the first qualification is to have two good eyes!" Know-It-All got to his feet and, aping One-Eye's manner of tossing his head back and forth, walked back under the eaves where Scabby Head and the rest of them were waiting.

Scabby Head didn't even look up at Know-It-All, but before he'd sat down, Fire Baby began to rail at him: "What the hell did you come back for?" The meaning behind this question escaped Know-It-All, who sat down ostentatiously. Fire Baby glared at him, then jabbed him with his elbow. "We don't need your kind over here!"

"Fuck you! A person with one eye is fiercer than those with two!" He still hadn't grasped the meaning behind Fire Baby's comments. "Society, society, corporation, society. Now what's bigger, society or a corporation? Do you know or not?" He paused for a moment. Actually, he didn't know himself. "If you want to know, I'll tell you. My hernia here is the biggest!" With that he took the wind out of the other man's sails.

Fire Baby laughed in spite of himself. He jabbed his elbow into Know-It-All, who turned around to look at him. Fire Baby's tone had lost its edge as he said, "What the hell did you come back for?"

Scabby Head cut in before Know-It-All had time to answer: "After this, if you line up on Han Qinzai's side, you don't have to come back over here." Know-It-All was stunned. "You've got to learn to choose between your friends and your enemies." Scabby

Head looked across the street, casting an icy look of warning from his seated position.

"Han Qinzai is an ambitious schemer." Fire Baby explained to Know-It-All the conclusions that he, Scabby Head, and the others had arrived at regarding Han Qinzai. Know-It-All bit his lower lip and nodded repeatedly, his eyes cast downward. "And so, don't let yourself be used. If Gold Clock and One-Eye want to go over there, that's their business. We don't care about them."

"That's right, he's a schemer," Know-It-All agreed.

"If he wasn't, then why didn't he hang around with us once he got here instead of walking all over the place by himself, doing whatever it is he does?" Fire Baby asked.

"That's the truth. I could see that too. Just a while ago when we came over here, he didn't want to stick with us but went over there across the street to be by himself."

"Then why did you go over there with him?"

"I just felt like chewing the fat, that's all."

"Open your eyes a little."

Know-It-All kept nodding his head. Blockhead was standing off to the side, giggling. Scabby Head was staring fixedly at Han Qinzai. Wanting to get into his good graces, Fire Baby commented, "Just look at Han Qinzai! I wonder what sort of scheme he's cooking up for us now?"

"You afraid of him?"

"Afraid of him, with you here? Afraid of a prick like that?"

Out of curiosity, they followed Han Qinzai's gaze.

"Hey!" Fire Baby poked Scabby Head and Know-It-All with his elbows. "Now I know what he's hatching in that head of his."

"I know that. Why do you think I've been watching him all this time?" Scabby Head narrowed his eyes as he glared at Han

Qinzai.

"I can tell too."

"Tell what?" Know-It-All asked.

"Just look at Han Qinzai."

"That lousy rat! Has he got his eye on Crazy Cai?"

"Now do you see?" Scabby Head said coldly. A feeling of uneasiness settled over the men. They stopped looking at Han Qinzai and, like him, riveted their attention on the madwoman, as a heated emotion gripped their hearts.

MAKE YOUR BEST MOVE

Scholar Yang's funeral procession, from the vanguard to the mourners, stretched a distance equivalent to thirty or forty shops.

Han Qinzai was one of the banner bearers, carrying a blue banner representing the great-grandchildren's generation. Immediately following him were Scholar Yang's image altar and his coffin. The mourners slowly made their way toward the busy part of town, and the men had heard that they were going to parade up and down several streets. Han Qinzai had a jittery feeling he couldn't shake. The route of the procession would surely take him past the stores owned by Stony, Prosperity, and Longevity. What if they spotted him? *Shit! They're sure to cut old Han Qinzai down! If I cover my face with the banner, the cloth is thin enough so that I can still see where I'm going.* This thought perked him up considerably, but as he walked on, a sudden apprehensiveness flashed into his mind. He quickly turned back to look at Scholar Yang's image altar. The expression in the clouded eyes of the portrait was still one of peace with the world. *I know I had nothing to do with this.* He looked back one more time. *Scholar Yang, go in peace.*

When the funeral procession passed by the open-air turntable, even though his face was completely hidden by the banner, Han Qinzai could still see Longevity's store behind the bobbing heads of the crowd of onlookers. Then he saw Longevity himself, dressed in a vest, his arms folded in front of his chest so that his tough, hardened muscles glistened in the sunlight. "Damn him!" he cursed under his breath. There was a distance of no more than ten steps or so between him and Longevity, and the worst thing was that they were on the same side of the street. Longevity was looking his way, his eyes fixed on Scholar Yang's image. Han Qinzai was afraid that Longevity would spot him. Then an idea popped into his head: he began to hobble along like a cripple. This so surprised Gold Clock, who was walking beside him, that for a moment he was speechless. Han Qinzai was now directly opposite Longevity; he closed his eyes and began to chant:

"Oh, Earth God, oh, Matsu, Goddess of the Sea, please bestow your protection on Han Qinzai." When he opened his eyes again, he was terrified to see that he had strayed from the procession and that the onlookers were laughing at him. He ran back like a shot, completely forgetting that he was supposed to be hobbling like a cripple. "Damn it!" He could all but feel Longevity's eyes on his back, and a shiver ran down his spine. He wished he hadn't feigned being a cripple. He wanted to rectify the situation, but as he walked down the crowded street, each time he decided to make things right, he found that somehow he lacked the determination he'd had when he first saw Longevity.

"Han Qinzai, what's wrong with your leg?" Gold Clock asked impulsively.

"Got a damned cramp in it."

"Oh! The poor damned legs!" Gold Clock's glance moved from Han Qinzai's leg up to his head. "Why are you covering your face like that?"

"Don't you feel the heat today?" He kept his face covered. "This makes me a lot cooler."

"Yeah, it's hotter than hell." Gold Clock covered his face the same way. "Hey, it *is* cooler!"

The dramatic troupe came clamoring down the road, tooting horns and beating drums, making a lot of noise. All together there were some twenty different types of musical instruments—the two-man great brass gong, the bass drum, the hand drums, cymbals, bells, trumpets, three-stringed fiddles, two-stringed violins, flutes—and the cacophony produced by all these instruments, which were being played for all they were worth, assaulted the ears of everyone within range. Without straining at all, Han Qinzai could hear the muffled sound of the gong as it was struck by one of the musicians at the head of the procession. That was the only other gong like the one now lying beneath his bed. He listened and he thought, and as he did so, the gong rang out loudly and blended in with his reveries.

> *Bong! Bong! Bong!*
> *The gong beater's coming your way—*
> *Listen everyone, here's what I have to say—*
> *A call for all pilgrims at the Qiding Temple of the Patriarch—*
> *Tomorrow afternoon at two o'clock—*
> *Fire dancers will be there, tallies will be drawn—*
> *Bong! Bong! Bong!*
> *Calling all the Buddhist faithful—*

Get ready your spirit money, your crackers, and your candles—
Everyone off to the Qiding Temple of the Patriarch to burn incense and bow to the gods—
Bong! Bong! Bong!
Listen carefully, one and all—
Women in their period, or pregnant, cannot go—
People in mourning cannot go—
Bong! Bong! Bong!
Everyone who goes will be given a tally—
To take home and paste over the door for protection—
Bong! Bong! Bong!

"Should we prepare a sacrifice?" a woman asked him.

"It's a lot better if you can. But if you've never made a vow for blessings received from the Patriarch, there's no need. All you need is spirit money, crackers, and candles."

"Is it okay to bring fruit?"

Han Qinzai found himself surrounded by the neighborhood women.

"Sure. Fruit and clear tea are fine, but it's important to go with a pure heart."

"Is it okay to go if you've had a baby within the month?"

"Oh! If the month's confinement isn't up, you're not clean, so you can't go."

"Did you say two o'clock? Two in the afternoon?"

"Two o'clock tomorrow afternoon." Han Qinzai was kept busy turning from one woman to another, answering all their questions.

If he didn't get away from them pretty soon, he thought as the number of women increased, he'd find himself answering the same questions over and over. He started beating his gong, made his way forward through an opening in the crowd, and walked off. Naturally, some of the people stayed behind to pass on the news about the Patriarch to the late arrivals, as though they had been invested with some authority.

*   *   *

Bong! Bong! Bong! Beneath the same bright sun, the heat of summer growing more intense, his reveries dissolved back into reality, and as he looked out through the cloth in front of his eyes to see the faces of all the people gathered to watch the festivities, each and every one of them familiar to him, he was truly frightened that someone might spot him carrying a funeral banner. He heaved a long sigh and the emotional excitement he'd been experiencing turned into a great, heavy stone that weighed down on him.

"Gold Clock," he called out. Gold Clock had long since stopped covering his face with the cloth banner. "Have you ever seen me out beating my gong?"

"I've… seen you, of course I have." He was walking with his legs far apart so as not to cause pain to his hernia.

"How'd you think I was at it?"

"I never could figure out why you gave it up." Gold Clock cocked his head to look over at him. Han Qinzai had by then already edged over to him until they were shoulder to shoulder. "Beating a gong has got to be a lot more dignified than carrying a funeral banner."

"Dignified, you say?" With his back to the man, Han Qinzai smiled an ambiguous smile; he didn't dare look at Gold Clock.

"Yeah! I just can't figure out why you'd give it up."

Han Qinzai laughed a dull laugh, which Gold Clock found even more difficult to figure out.

The reverberations from the gong, almost illusory in effect, floated in waves of scorching heat and reached Han Qinzai's ears in pulsations. Thus it went until the entire procession was gathered at the oil shop at the end of the street, leaving room for the pallbearers to carry their burden into the cemetery. The banner carriers were resting on their haunches beneath a red banyan tree. Scabby Head coughed dryly several times, then cursed, "Shit! Well, we're all here. Scabby Head, Rotten Ear, One-Eye, Gold Clock, and the Cripple. Have I missed anyone?" It suddenly dawned on Han Qinzai that what he was holding in his hand was not a gong mallet.

"Don't forget me, Blockhead! Hee hee..." Blockhead added his name to the list, which broke the others up and lightened their mood. As for Han Qinzai, this round of laughter seemed to isolate him off to one side, and the barren scene before him produced an anguish that no amount of appeasement could drive away. He was beset by self-pity that had lost all its significance. Feeling terribly depressed, he was thinking that the only way to remove his anguish was to show contempt for these men. With this decision, their every action, the way they had isolated him, nothing could bring him any pain. *A bunch of old bums, lower than pigs!* he cursed inwardly. But he was still put out of sorts by their laughter. He raised his hand to rub his chest, then said, looking for sympathy, "Mongrel, you guys really hurt me—I'm still sore." He followed this with another inward curse: *They're worse than pigs.*

"What's that? Didn't they turn you into a cripple?" Scabby

Head queried in mock seriousness.

"I'm sore all over."

"Hey, Mongrel, he says you banged him with your head so hard he hurts all over. Go a little easier next time, Mongrel, Fire Baby!" Scabby Head nodded with satisfaction as the other men burst out laughing, having understood the intent of his comments.

No matter what, it's a lot better to argue with them than just sit here all by myself. So he fired off one comment after another, though nothing came of any of it and their interest flagged. In the midst of his bewilderment, he suddenly thought of some dirty stories that rescued him from his predicament.

Eventually Scabby Head broke in on his story. "Han Qinzai, the musicians are coming back. How much longer is this story of yours? Why not wrap it up for now and finish it some other time."

The words "some other time" were particularly pleasing to Han Qinzai's ear, so he stood up and brought his story to an end. "Of course, you all know that when the woman lay down in the grass, her bound feet, which were sticking up in the air, kept moving up and down, until her husband saw them and shouted happily: 'Amei! I caught the turkey! I caught the turkey! I can see its head.'" He still held his audience, and even though they got to their feet, picked up their banners, and fell in behind the musicians in a big hurry to get back to Scholar Yang's home for a free meal, Know-It-All, Mongrel, and some of the others pushed Gold Clock out of the way to move up alongside Han Qinzai and hear some more of his stories. But all the while they kept an eye on Scabby Head, watching the expression on his face.

"Han Qinzai," Scabby Head said with a smile as he turned to look behind him, "these guys can't hold on to their money as it is, and if you keep it up, tomorrow they'll all be broke."

Know-It-All and the others detected a note of approval from Scabby Head that they were with Han Qinzai. So Gold Clock pushed by the others, yelling, "So you want to listen, do you? Well, so do I!" Han Qinzai's heart was warming up. His mouth was split in a broad grin and he was laughing, though not a sound emerged. His face looked as if it had been stamped by the rays of the sun.

THE NIGHTMARE

After several uneventful days had passed, everything returned to normal: the second rice harvest had been completed, and no dreams invaded his sleep. His life had taken on a fixed routine: rising with the sun, he prepared a simple breakfast, then went over to the kadang tree, joined the funeral banquets, argued, chatted amiably; meanwhile resentment filled his heart more and more deeply. Even his limited supply of dirty stories had been exhausted, and it was unnecessary for him to observe the cold looks in the others' eyes or listen to their conversation to know that in this circle he had lost that certain something. If the situation didn't improve, before too long it wouldn't make much difference whether he was here or not. But what could he do? he asked himself. He'd been born a person of integrity, and there was no way he, Han Qinzai, could stoop to supporting another man's balls as he crossed a threshold! *Who does Scabby Head think he is? I wouldn't even let him wash my feet.* He was fighting mad, and the more he thought about it, the more his heart froze. Every time Han Qinzai's turn to help in the kitchen rolled around, Scabby Head and the others said that he wasn't a real member of the group, so they skipped him and went on to the next in line. Whenever Know-It-All returned from helping in the kitchen, in obvious high spirits, he'd make a big show of saying to the others in front of him, "Wa! There was a piece of lean meat this big," using his hands to describe it. Or he'd say, "I dipped it in soy sauce and in garlic paste and had it with a bottle of wine—oh, shit! Just imagine eating like that every day!" As he carried on, his eyes never left Han Qinzai.

Ptui! *These guys were all raised by pigs, and this big liar here is saying, "Hai! Just think what it would be like!" Fuck him and all his ancestors! Why don't you guys go to the open-air stalls in front of the Temple of the Patriarch to ask about me, about my good old days? What makes you think a lousy piece of lean meat would be such a temptation to Han Qinzai? That makes me laugh. Back in those days, whenever I went to the Temple of the Patriarch, Pine Root, Woody, and Righteous Virtue would call out to me, asking me this and that, to get on my good side. They'd shout, "Han Qinzai, we've already warmed some wine for you." "Han Qinzai, we've got some goose liver here for you." Hmph! I serve no master, and if I feel like it I can eat sharkskin!*

Bong! Bong! Bong! Somewhere along the line, it seemed, a gong had come to exist in his mind. It resounded—*bong! bong!*—on its own. In the middle of the night it was so persistent it caused him great uneasiness and made his ears ring. He sat up straight, his nerves so taut his eyes fluttered. He looked at the darkness around him, as if he wanted to stare a hole in it to get a better look. He felt the walls close in tightly around him and eventually realized that he knew the source of this pressure: the darkness was congealing into a hard lump and was about to freeze him solid there in the shelter. He breathed with difficulty until, from the depths of his confusion, with an agility born of terror, he leaped frantically off his bamboo bed. As he knocked over two empty bottles, the noise tore through the oppressively thick atmosphere, which quickly swallowed the sound up again. He stumbled headlong through the shelter entrance, his outstretched arms supporting him against the concrete walls. "Come here!" he yelled. "Scabby Head, if you've any guts, come here! Come here, all of you! Fuck you all!" His neck strained to support his drooping head when suddenly he felt the cool air of an autumn night, and just as suddenly the faces of the men under the kadang tree appeared superimposed on his mind, particularly their cold, hard eyes; he was powerless to drive away those looks. "I told you to come! Didn't you hear me? If you had any guts you'd have come!" Lines of laughter showed in the corners of their eyes.

"If you don't believe me, there's nothing I can do. But don't look at me that way. Let's hear you say something. Let it out, curse me if you want to."

But they just sat there lazily, though they continued to look at him coldly, occasionally exchanging glances among themselves.

Han Qinzai looked at each of them in turn but could not detect the trace of a kind look.

"You all know well enough how Crazy Cai was deflowered beneath the pork butcher's counter in the marketplace. I felt sorry for her, that's all." A look of exasperation that confused the men appeared on his face. "What do you want me to say? I feel sorry for her."

The others glanced at Scabby Head, who smiled. They turned their cold eyes back on Han Qinzai as they heard him mutter, "I know why you guys are suspicious of me: you're thinking about how I give her food whenever we have a funeral banquet, and how I do it on the sly. I know you won't believe what I say, but I just feel sorry for her." He saw that they were looking at one another, conversing with their eyes. "But," he continued, "I did it on the sly because I was afraid you guys would get the wrong idea. In all good conscience, may heaven strike me down with lightning if there's been anything between me and that woman."

But no matter how sincerely he said it, opening up his very heart to show them, knowing glances passed among the men, giving him an even more unpleasant taste in his mouth.

"I really didn't do a lowdown thing like that!" He felt as if he were being tortured into self-revelations, one after another, under the unchanging looks of doubt in their eyes. He continued, "You all want me to own up to it, but…" He stopped, finding it difficult to say what was on his mind. This created a moment of tense anticipation. Finally, in nervous embarrassment, he admitted, "If it's my thoughts you want to know, well, it did occur to me several times, but when the time came and I saw her, I ran away, afraid to go through with it. I might have had the same thing on my mind when I took the food over to her, but the moment I laid eyes on her, I just put the bowl down on the ground, turned, and ran off. I was thinking of her. I *was* thinking of her!" This came out almost unintelligibly and had something of a sob about it. Scabby Head and the others laughed. Sensing that he was still not believed, he cited another instance. "The night before last, she came to the park alone late at night—it must've been at least eleven o'clock, when the place was deserted." Clarity suddenly came to his voice and his mood grew somber. The faces of the men around him were frozen with the attentiveness of people listening fearfully to a ghost story, unwilling to miss a single word. "When I saw her, I was scared and pleased at the same time. I looked all around to make sure we were alone. 'Crazy Cai,' I said to her, 'you come with me to the air-raid shelter and I'll give you something to eat.' And she did, she followed me quietly back to the shelter. I was really getting the itch then. I looked around again, and there was no one, not even a stray dog." When he reached this point in his narration, the other men began to squirm uneasily, as if they would burst waiting for the climax.

"Now you all know that even though Crazy Cai's got a big belly, she still isn't bad. I was constantly on the alert to see if there was anyone nearby. Although she seemed to know what I had in mind, she didn't resist. I figured she needed it too, since she already had some experience. As the saying goes: 'A man enjoys it three parts, a woman seven.' When I was sure we were alone, I... I reached out and touched her arm, but then I drew back like my hand had been struck by lightning. I give you my word—all this time that she's been on my mind, the night before last was the first time I touched her." His listeners' faces showed how displeased they were that his narration wasn't going into enough detail. "I started to get scared," he went on, "and I told her to leave—started pushing her away, in fact—but not only did she stay where she was, she even headed into the air-raid shelter by herself, which scared me so much I just climbed up onto the grass covering and waited there anxiously till dawn."

When Scabby Head and the others heard this, they showed their utter disgust, born of disappointment and a sense of having been cheated, with looks that seemed to mean that they wouldn't give him the satisfaction of getting angry. And their disappointment proved a disappointment to him.

"I *did* think of her," he yelled. "Who hasn't? I'll bet all of you have. But that's all it was—thoughts. If you say I was wrong, then the only thing I did wrong was touch her once two nights ago. But I let go of her right away. I really did. Because I was too scared!"

At this point, not only was he subjected to icy stares, he was also the target of silent looks of bitter loathing. He voiced his feelings of injustice by yelling, "If you don't believe me, you can call her over and ask her yourself! If anything happened between her and me, you can do anything you want to! You can take me around to all the town gates, where I'll beat my gong and admit my guilt in front of everyone. How's that?"

Scabby Head expressed all their sentiments with a hateful snort. As far as Han Qinzai was concerned, that was an ambiguous response. He was feeling terribly dejected, unable to understand why he had to give these men so many explanations. He regretted having told them about the incident of the night before last, and of having let out his secret thoughts for Crazy Cai. In sum, he regretted having said any of this to these men.

* * *

Han Qinzai bought two bottles of 25-proof cheap wine and headed home to his air-raid shelter, making up his mind once again not to go back, ever. *Who cares that there'll be food to eat tomorrow at the funeral at Kelin! I'll just drink these two bottles of wine and get a good night's sleep.* He was mentally exhausted to the point that all desires had left him. He just hid in his shelter and drowned his sorrows in the wine. Before he passed out, the mosquitoes that were feeding on him had all fallen drunkenly to the ground without even getting their fill of his blood. A kerosene lamp constructed of a tie band from a pair of shorts, lying in a small plate and supported by a single split chopstick, burned unwaveringly all the way down to the plate, until the supply of kerosene was exhausted.

The sound of a gong being struck resounded in his ears, but no matter how hard he tried, he could not lift his head. It drooped forward until it could go no farther, and then it rolled back again. In like fashion, no matter how hard he tried, he could not wipe away the persistent images of those cold looks. It eventually got so bad they gave him shivers. Things had deteriorated with Han Qinzai until all he could do was shout in confusion, "Come on! Go ahead and look, what good does that do? Anyone, anyone with any guts, come over here…." He waved his arm in the air, causing him to lose his equilibrium as he stumbled several steps out the door. He lay prostrate on the grass, continuing to mumble in an unbroken stream. He was soothed by gust after gust of cool night air in the open park. Like an infant sleeping soundly at its mother's breast, he noiselessly sucked in the breath of life.

* * *

A road, the most familiar one of all, stretched out before him. Faces so familiar that there was no longer any need to consciously record their names lined the brightly lit roadsides, eagerly awaiting the public announcement of some vile deed committed in town. With this sight in front of him, Han Qinzai balked. The gong felt so heavy he could barely hold it; even the mallet seemed heavy as a boulder. His mind was busily engaged in reflecting on ways of dying. He gave it some serious thought for a while but found that he lacked both the knowledge and the courage. He realized that there were things more fearful than death. But all these impressions, ill defined though they were, took the shape of a torturous anxiety. He turned back to beg for mercy but, seeing pair after pair of staring, frightening eyes, he was rendered mute. Turning back around, he felt those cold glares bore into him until his backbone seemed to recoil. Apparently the only option open to him was to follow through on his vow. At this critical moment, he still had thoughts of changing the wording of his defense, but no matter how simple he made it or how reserved, he would still have to say something along these lines: "The gong beater's coming your way. Listen everyone, here's what I have to say: I, Han Qinzai, have committed the unpardonable sin of seducing Crazy Cai...." He wanted badly to beg for mercy, or for death. Met by the same cold, unrelenting stares, he had no choice but to screw up his courage and walk forward, beating his gong and shouting, "The gong beater's coming your way. Listen everyone, here's what I have to say: I, I..." He could not go on, as the full awareness of his discomfort hit him.

His mind was still clouded and confused when he opened his eyes, and he was in a state of total shock. He had no idea why he had walked into the woods—then it gradually dawned on him that the rice stalks that rose unevenly around him as he lay on the ground had made him believe he was in the woods. As he reached a state of awareness, the first emotion he experienced was the self-congratulatory happiness of someone who realizes that a calamity has turned out to be only a nightmare. But this short-lived happiness only increased the mournfulness of his self-pity.

Today was the grand funeral of the rich man, Chen from Kelin, and there would be food to eat. He'd heard that the Chen family owned nearly ten acres of land. Han Qinzai was through making vows. He wanted to go over to the kadang tree. *If they don't believe me,* he thought as he walked, *then they don't believe* me—*if the roots of the tree are solid, there's no need for the branches to fear a typhoon. How could people like that ever understand me, Han Qinzai? They think I'm the same as them. That makes me laugh! Like that episode yesterday, when Scabby Head and the others gave me those cold glares.* He was not going to give that a second thought. His thoughts moved to the rich Mr. Chen's ten acres of land, the golden grain, the piles of money, the funeral arrangements, the meat on the tables, the generous packets of spending money. And even if the image of Scabby Head and the others should occasionally flash into his mind, he had only to silently curse, *Fuck them*, and that took care of that. As he passed over Southgate Bridge, the canopy of the kadang tree came into view once again. His thoughts having turned to the tree, he spat on the ground. "Ptui! Fuck them!"

THE RAINBOW WITH NO END

"Ah!" Mongrel seemed to be trying to wrap up all of their comments into a general conclusion. "'In shallow water the dragon is laughed at by the shrimps; in the open plain the tiger is at the mercy of dogs.'"

"What's that?" Know-It-All jumped up shouting. "Is that an admission that he's a dragon or a tiger? And we're a bunch of little shrimps and mutts? If you don't know how to make comparisons, then keep your mouth shut. You're the mutt, and who wants to be associated with you?"

The others all looked at Know-It-All and nodded, some voicing their agreement with "That's right!" or "Good point!"

"Ai! Why make such a big deal out of it? Why do that? I'm only here on a temporary basis, you know." Gold Clock the herniated was making fun of Han Qinzai by mimicking his manner of speaking. He glanced at Scabby Head, then at the others. He was seldom in such high spirits, for it seemed that he never did anything right in the presence of these men. But this time, not only did he escape being yelled at and called "Hernia," he was actually rewarded by their lighthearted approval. "Temporary, I say, just temporary. You know what I mean?"

"Oh, no, don't be temporary! Stay here with us," Mongrel cut in, like an actor on the stage.

But Gold Clock was so beside himself with the joy of not having angered the others that he completely missed the opportunity to engage Mongrel in a mock debate. He just sat there, his arms clasped around his knees, as he rocked back and forth. Mongrel was growing a little impatient, but before the moment had passed, Fire Baby said, in imitation of Han Qinzai:

"No, no, when I say temporary I mean temporary. I'm not like you guys." He had all of Han Qinzai's little movements down pat, and the others laughed at him. They constantly looked over to see if there was any reaction from Han Qinzai. As if he had some magnetic effect that kept drawing their eyes back to him, they seemed powerless to keep from looking his way.

Han Qinzai sat alone in the spot where normally they all sat in a group; while the others had picked up and moved to a spot under another kadang tree, some three or four trees removed from him. Their conversation was intended to drive him away. Their every sentence reached his ears and penetrated deeply into his heart. It was all over for him, he thought. His only recourse was to stay put, whether they wanted him there or not, and see what they would do. He shrugged off the knowledge that it was a very undignified way to go about it. Each time a peal of laughter floated across, he was driven by his curiosity to turn around and see what was happening. But with all the strength he could muster, he forced his will upon his seemingly rebellious neck. When all he could hear was a series of unintelligible mutterings, broken suddenly by an explosion of laughter, the strain was so intense that a soreness developed in his neck. He rested the point of his chin between his knees as he squatted there, not allowing his curiosity to get the better of him. He simply didn't know how else to handle the situation. More than once he was so agitated by what they were saying that he was on the verge of jumping to his feet and cursing them soundly before walking off and washing his hands of them. But for reasons even he did not know, he was unable to jump up, powerless to curse out loud. He just stayed as he was, squatting motionlessly on his haunches, until his buttocks, his legs, and his back were numb with soreness and eventually all that was left to him was the remorseful anger that filled his still-alert mind.

He made up his mind that if he heard any more talk or laughter that distressed him he'd leave at once. But immediately after making this decision, he heard Mongrel say something about "hatching an egg." This produced a round of side-splitting laughter. His resolve of a moment before slipped away and lay there steaming. He began talking to himself. *I'm not stupid! Leave? That's exactly what they want. So I'll stay put and see what they do about it.* He hugged his knees more tightly. Fearing that he wouldn't be able to follow through with his latest resolution, he forced his chin down hard, closed his eyes, and, with all the willpower he could muster, resisted whatever it was that enervated him; thrills of victory came in waves to salve his wounded heart, which in turn inspired him with greater courage to continue the struggle. This in turn increased his fatigue while simultaneously causing him to experience the intoxication of a tragic hero as he held on to this particular spot.

Another burst of laughter hit him like a bayonet thrust. *Could they be laughing at me because I've got no guts? Fuck them! To hell with them! What can they do if I don't leave? So what if I don't have any guts? No! I don't have any guts if I do leave.* Right! I don't have any guts if I do leave. He hugged his knees tightly, pressed his chin down hard, and closed his eyes as the *bong, bong* sound of a gong rang in his ears. Nowhere, not on any street or lane of the town, was there a cruel face or a pair of cold, expressionless eyes. His throat was as parched as if he'd been shouting at the top of his lungs. He noticed that his hands were hanging loosely, as if the left one were holding a gong, the right one grasping a mallet, and both quivering slightly. After hurriedly and forcefully stopping these involuntary movements, he glanced at the thumb of his left hand, which was roughly stroking the callus on the inside of his index finger. This callus had been caused by the constant rubbing of the rope handle of the gong he had once carried. He smiled grimly.

As for Scabby Head and the others, although they'd gained the upper hand by expelling Han Qinzai from the group, now as they watched him sit there so composed, apparently unaffected by what they were saying, conflicting emotions of triumph and defeat assailed them as well. The only difference was the source of these emotions: for them it came from a sense of superiority; for him, from one of inferiority. It was a stalemate. As it turned out, Han Qinzai was able to minimize the effects of this particular stalemate, for he had analyzed his own present situation and the deterioration of what had originally been good relations with the others. Scabby Head and the rest, on the other hand, after spending a good part of the day poking fun and directing heated criticisms at Han Qinzai, found that he was unaffected by it all. Eventually, without being aware of it, they began to lose interest, even though no one was willing to bring the episode to a close. So they let things run their course, waiting for their interest to peter out naturally. Even the comments of Mongrel, Fire Baby, and Know-It-All, who continued to take their pleasure in heatedly baiting and poking fun at him, could no longer get a rise out of the other men. Gradually they too quieted down. But they didn't let Han Qinzai off the hook completely, for in addition to openly isolating him, they were already contemplating what they would subject him to next. In the meantime, Han Qinzai was no longer exposed to the laughter that had so unsettled him.

Suddenly a new thought disturbed him as he sat there in solitude. *What would happen if someone came now to make funeral arrangements? Should I go along with the others? Or shouldn't I? If not, why sit here and suffer? Wouldn't I feel a lot better if I stood up and gave them hell, then just walked away? If I were to go along with these heartless bums, who knows what trouble they might dream up for me?* He thought and he thought, but to no avail. Concerned that some bereaved family member might turn up across the street to buy a coffin, he hoped desperately that at least it wouldn't happen today.

A leaf from the kadang tree fell to the ground in front of him. He felt like someone who had run into a friend so intimate that all formalities could be dispensed with, someone he could welcome or ignore, as he pleased. He looked at it lazily, then picked it up and put it up to his mouth to lick it. He focused his gaze on the leaf until his eyes grew crossed; his face was gaunt and slack. His thoughts turned to his present predicament, the source of which could be traced initially to the death of Scholar Yang. But it was his relationship with Crazy Cai that had had the most direct effect. At first it had been a simple misunderstanding. But after her belly had begun to swell, things started to turn bad. *What a joke! Blockhead can do it, so why can't I? Besides, I only* thought *about it.* More giggling from Blockhead's pursed lips, but he couldn't tell if it came from across the way or was a figment of his imagination.

Blockhead was giggling. "Don't, Mongrel. My ears are splitting."

"Tell us, what did you do with Crazy Cai?"

"Don't. What did I do?" Blockhead stammered. "I… I only… I only took a piss in her, that's all." Mongrel let go of Blockhead's hand, joining the others in side-splitting laughter. After that, whenever they wanted to have a laugh at Blockhead's expense, they had only to grab hold of one of his ears and ask him what he'd done with Crazy Cai. He would say that he'd taken a piss in her, that's all. Later on, merely grabbing his ear would make him blurt out the same thing without even being asked the question.

One day, Scabby Head suddenly asked, "Han Qinzai, haven't you really ever had anything to do with Crazy Cai?"

"Me?" Han Qinzai was momentarily speechless. Then he giggled and said, "I only took a piss in her, that's all."

At first a few of them chuckled at this, but when they saw the hardened looks on the faces of Scabby Head and one or two of the others, the laughter died as quickly as it had begun. What had been intended as a joke had backfired, resulting in Han Qinzai's complete isolation from that day on.

Crazy Cai's belly had now become *the* topic of conversation among most of the people in town, particularly the women. Han Qinzai was terribly worried that his name would be drawn into the talk. Therefore, bearing his vague anguish as best he could, he stopped bringing her food. And yet, she continued to greet him with that idiotic smile of hers whenever she saw him.

He had unconsciously chewed the kadang leaf into a pulpy mass, and the slightly bitter juice from the leaf entered his stomach, swallow by swallow. He thought, without being totally aware of it, that if that piece of growing flesh inside Crazy Cai's belly was his, then... *Wa! Wouldn't that be something! I, Han Qinzai, would gladly jump into a vat of boiling oil if I had a child. I could endure any amount of suffering. That heartless woman of mine; if she'd had any feelings at all, Ahui would be over twenty by now. Shit! But then, what good would have come of it? It served her right, being killed by that guy. It just proves the saying that evil is repaid with evil, good rewarded with good; nothing is left unrecompensed, and your day will surely come.* This thought served to smooth away the feelings of injustice that filled his heart. Except for the sense of isolation they produced, the clamorous sounds that floated over to him were no longer a cause of concern. The rules of Heaven were the guiding principle in the ways of life. He who obstructs another person will be visited by heavenly reprisals. He believed strongly in this principle of retribution and was convinced that in the future, Scabby Head and the others would get their just deserts. This brought a momentary feeling of comfort to him, and the melancholia caused by fleeting memories of past incidents was swept cleanly away, while the inner strength he had mastered in his struggles dissipated. At this moment, he felt himself truly at rest—body and soul.

"Han Qinzai—" A strange sound from Scabby Head's direction came to him. As though shaken out of a sleep, he looked over his shoulder, where he saw Mongrel jerking his chin upward and pointing his nose at him, saying to a neatly dressed man, "Isn't that him over there?" All the men, including the stranger, turned their eyes in the direction Mongrel was indicating to look at Han Qinzai. This threw a slight scare into him. The man stepped onto the pedal of his bicycle and pushed himself over toward Han Qinzai.

"Han Qinzai, are you still beating your gong?"

He couldn't believe his ears. He got to his feet, feeling both flabbergasted and elated. Stooping slightly, he didn't know what to do with his hands, putting them first behind his back, then clasping them in front of him. "Do you mean…" he asked cautiously. But before he'd gotten the words out, the other man butted in impatiently, "Well, yes or no?"

"Yes, yes, yes," Han Qinzai replied with a sense of urgency. "Mm-hm, mm-hm!" Although he didn't know what the man had in mind, he didn't dare ask any more questions.

"Meet me at the district headquarters at two tomorrow afternoon. I've got a job for you." Then he added impatiently, "I'll need your services for three days."

"Yes, yes, yes…" Han Qinzai stammered, nodding with each word. He kept it up until the man was out of sight. Then it came to him—the district headquarters. No wonder the man looked so familiar; in the past, he was the one who had always hired him when the district headquarters had an announcement. "This head of mine is really something—I even forgot him." As he watched the man's retreating figure, the gratitude and happiness brought by this unexpected opportunity had the effect of slowly straightening his slightly crooked back, like a vine growing at night. Enough time passed while he was in this state of mind to vex the men looking on; then, sensing something in the air, he became aware of several pairs of eyes staring at his back. But there were no more cold shivers up his spine. He coughed dryly, sending the stares back where they came from, then turned around and gave the others a sweeping glance. Much to his surprise, these men whom he had endured for so long, whom he had feared to anger, and whose arrogance he had catered to now resembled little more than a mass of dead cinders. Some of them were blinking involuntarily. Sickened by what he saw, Han Qinzai opened his mouth and released his long-pent-up anger.

"What's wrong with you? Look! Don't you know who I am? Since you want to look, get yourselves an eyeful. I'm different from bums like you, who spend your whole lives gnawing on coffin boards!" So saying, he rolled his sleeves up, and with his arms—both as thin as rails—at his waist, he struck the pose of a scarecrow. Suddenly realizing that this outburst had included him in its invective, he added, "Don't you get the idea that I'm a bum like the rest of you. Maybe I'll just go marry Crazy Cai, and what of it! If I want to take a piss, I'll take a piss, and what of it! I'll take it wherever I want to, and what can you do about it? All you can do is swallow your own spit." And yet for some reason, they still intimidated him. Almost instinctively, he maintained a guarded distance of as much as three or four kadang trees from them.

Scabby Head and the others were speechless, looking as if someone had smashed something valuable of theirs when they weren't looking, and they didn't know what to do about it. At the same time, they were struck by the feeling that a livelihood of gnawing on coffin boards really wasn't a very respectable occupation (prior to this, the thought had evidently never crossed their minds). This impression, however, was only a shallow, fleeting one, and did not enter their relative consciousness. Self-demeaning looks appeared on their faces, but these were nothing more than instinctive shows of self-protection meant to elicit sympathy and help them over this critical moment.

Marry Crazy Cai? This shocked even Han Qinzai. How could he have said that? He felt a need to explain, both to himself and to the others. "I …" He sputtered for a while, but could never get past the word "I." Finally, growing impatient with himself, he blurted out, "I, Han Qinzai, mean what I say. If I say temporary, I mean temporary. My teeth aren't made to gnaw on coffin boards like yours are." But no matter how satisfying all this was, he couldn't shake the emotional discomfort caused by his comment about marrying Crazy Cai. He was afraid they'd take it in all of its despicability and turn it on him. "Of course, I wouldn't actually marry her; what I meant was if I did, what could you guys do about it?" But that didn't make him feel any better. *If I feel like marrying her, that's what I'll do! Having a baby is easy, but rearing a child is a deed of kindness; anyone can father a child, but a parent is one who rears a child, whoever's seed it may be!*

Among the group of men, only Blockhead was a loner, totally unconcerned about what earthshaking incident might be occurring in this circle; he simply continued doing what he did best, which was to giggle foolishly. But on this occasion, he was unable to draw any laughter from the others.

I've got to hurry back and get everything ready. I'll have to polish the gong with ashes, and the mallet—I may not be able to find it at all, and even if I do, the cloth head has probably rotted away. But the thought that he was going to let these men off so easily was an irritation, and he was tempted to level one more hateful blast at them. He thought for a moment, then said:

"You guys come over to my place when you're not busy. I won't be able to provide too much, but at least you can have some rice wine and smoke a cigarette or two—no problem there. Now I mean it—you come on over. Han Qinzai will be waiting for you." His intent was to mock them, and as he saw the embarrassed looks on their faces, he knew he'd accomplished his goal. He spat once loudly, then turned briskly on his heel and walked off.

Later on, if I can really manage it, I'll treat them to a sumptuous meal in one of the open-air stalls in front of the Temple of the Patriarch. Then I'll give them each a pack of Long Life cigarettes and see if that doesn't make them feel just terrible.

THE GONG GOES *BONG! BONG! BONG!*

"Hey, it's time to get up." He stretched and reached beneath the bed to take out the gong that he'd been using as a catchall. He examined it carefully. "Wow, you sure have slept for a long time; you've even got a dead lizard in here!" He stared intently at the sunken eyes with the tiny specks of white showing through the lizard's skin. Then he picked out a nail from the junk inside and used it to flip the lizard's carcass onto the floor, after which he turned the gong upside down and dumped everything into a heap under his bed. At that moment he realized that he was holding in his hand a real but badly tarnished gong, and his heart was pounding uncontrollably. He turned the gong over and over in his hands, brushing the dust off as he did. He spat on it, then rubbed it with his fingers as he walked out of the shelter. He examined it carefully once more in the natural light, as the sun glinted weakly off the spots he'd rubbed with saliva. He could envision the gong in all its shiny luster; its sound, which was in his mind always, seemed now to be pounding in his ears.

Bong! Bong! Bong! "The gong beater's coming your way..." He muttered under his breath, "Once I fall on better days I'll show them. Where do they get off looking down on me?" He'd pulled up a handful of wild grass from atop the air-raid shelter; with it he scooped up some ashes from the incinerator, then gently rubbed the face of the gong. Although it had the scars of two cracks as wide as grains of rice where the hanging straps went, they'd been carefully polished so that when the gong was struck the sound wouldn't reveal any trace of the flaw, nor would its resonance be affected.

"Shit! Damned good-for-nothing!" He remembered the day those cracks appeared as if it were yesterday. It was on the day of the Matsu festival: following the procession, he'd been asked to stay over for a meal by the family selected to keep the goddess at the house for the year. He must have drunk a great deal that night, or else how could his gong have fallen on a cobblestone? Never before, in all the time he'd been beating the gong, had Han Qinzai dropped it. He'd replaced the rope straps about once a month. *What a damned good-for-nothing!* As he polished the gong, he cursed to himself, although only he knew what was being cursed.

As the gong began to shine once again, the lost days of Han Qinzai's past returned in all their vividness, giving a scintillating boost to his spirits. He reflected on how, because of the cracks in the gong, he had manipulated his wrist action as he wielded the mallet and struck the gong at just the right spot so that the sound had the same beauty and resonance as when it had been whole and perfect, and so that the cracks did not grow any longer. He knew the course of these two cracks by heart: they'd meet near the middle; then a tiny triangular section of brass, about one fifth of the gong, would fall off. In the past he'd taken pains to guard against this eventuality, and he would have to continue doing so from now on. As he relished these thoughts of the past, his wrist twitched involuntarily. He could see his reflection in the gong. He laughed inwardly.

"Oh-oh!" He raised his head to discover that someone was standing there watching him. This stunned him momentarily. "What time is it?"

"I don't know exactly; I just came from the marketplace. I noticed by the clock at the district headquarters that it was about eleven-thirty."

"How long ago was that?"

"I just came from there. Why? You back to beating the gong?"

"If I didn't, who would?"

"What's the occasion?"

"You can be sure there's an occasion. You go and tell everyone to keep their ears open." He saw another fellow—a young man—walking down the road. He stood up and called out, "Hey, elder brother!" The young man turned around. "Elder brother, do you have the time?"

"No, I don't," he said, shaking his head. "I'm on my way home to eat lunch."

"Eat lunch? Then it must be somewhere around noon," he said to himself, greatly relieved.

Returning to the shelter, he got some rags and his old mallet handle, then went outside into the sunlight, where he began making a mallet head. Every once in a while he asked the time of day from a passerby, and by the time he'd formed the mallet head out of the rags, he'd already asked three people. Time seemed to be standing still. He looked for but could not find a piece of hemp to twist into a strap for the gong; then he was reminded of the tie band that served as a belt. He hadn't used it long, so it was still serviceable. He went back into the shelter to get the tie band from his black trousers, which were draped over the head of his bed.

He knew he ought to eat something, but he wasn't the least bit hungry. He had brief thoughts of life under the kadang tree, of Crazy Cai, and of the days that were to come, but all these were cut short and superseded by the presence of "two o'clock" in his consciousness. Before actually meeting that man at the district headquarters at two o'clock, there was nothing else he could concentrate on. Should he go at one-thirty to wait for the man? No, one o'clock would be even safer.

Having reached the district headquarters gate well ahead of the appointed hour, Han Qinzai paced back and forth in front. He watched the people returning to work inside, one after another, until he grew a bit anxious. Just about everyone who worked there had returned, so where was the man who had agreed to meet him? Toying with the idea of going inside to ask around, he found he was much too frightened to do so.

"Han Qinzai!" someone called out from behind. He turned around, and there was the man. He told him he'd been there for an hour already, but the man, devoid of expression, simply told Han Qinzai to follow him.

"Are you all set?"

"I was all set a long time ago."

"Didn't you bring your gong?"

"I'll get it right away."

"No need." Every word the man spoke to Han Qinzai was uttered with a total absence of emotion, as if he were impatient with him. Han Qinzai was so guarded he didn't even dare breathe hard. "You see this thing?" the man said as he pointed to a placard leaning against a wall, on which some words were written. (The thing was made of tin.) "Well, I want you to carry it around and beat your gong. Do you know what it says?" For the first time he was looking directly at Han Qinzai, who forced a smile and shook his head, embarrassed. "Okay, then you just announce that this year's property tax and income tax are due by the end of the month."

"Yes, yes, I understand: the propriety tax and…"

"What do you mean, 'propriety tax'? Hmph! I'm not talking about taking a woman to a hotel for some hanky-panky, you know," the man said, unable to keep from smiling. But he quickly regained his composure and said with a scowl, "It's 'property,' not 'propriety.'"

"Oh! Property, property," Han Qinzai repeated with great effort.

"Right! Property, hm?"

"Excuse me," Han Qinzai said, cautiously trying to get into the man's good graces, "do I have to pay property taxes?"

"How should I know? Do you own a home?" he asked impatiently.

"I live in an air-raid shelter, the one in the park."

"Then you ought to pay an air-raid tax," the man answered, holding back his laughter by closing his mouth tightly.

"When is that due?"

"Ai, what a chatterbox! Just go out and beat your gong and we'll let you off the hook."

Han Qinzai's response was an embarrassed smile.

"How much do you want for three days' work, beginning this afternoon?"

"Don't worry about that." He didn't mind making sacrifices this time, for what mattered was that the man hire him again. "Forget it; I'll take whatever you want to give!"

"I can't do that."

"Then make it the same as I got in the past, and we won't count this afternoon."

"In the past?" The man reflected for a moment as Han Qinzai lifted up the placard, rested it on his shoulder, and started to walk off.

"Hey, hold on, wait a moment. Do you remember what you're supposed to say?"

"I know. 'This year's property tax and income tax are due by the end of the month.'"

"Now, that's 'property,' not 'propriety'! Remember that. Okay, go ahead and start."

Han Qinzai walked off carrying the tin banner, which made a twanging noise in the air. The feeling this gave him was nothing like the one he'd experienced from carrying funeral banners. He was struck by the changing fortunes of life: when luck was not with you, it was like being tied in a knot that could not be undone; the more you tried to free yourself, the more tightly you were bound. But when fortune smiled on you, like a magician's sleight of hand, one-two-three-presto! and all the loosened ends of the rope were laid out in straight lines.

Fortune did not smile upon a man many times in his lifetime, so it was essential that Han Qinzai take full advantage of his prospects this time. He had to make sure that his services would be needed in the future by producing greater results with his gong than the loudspeaker pedicab ever could. Over the next two and a half days, he thought, his beating the gong to urge the populace to pay their taxes ought to result in everyone in town's doing so by the end of the month. *I know what makes these people tick: if they think they can put it off, they will, and if they can get by with forgetting it altogether, they'll do that too. For people like this, who never cry until they actually see the coffin, the only way is to scare the hell out of them.*

Indian summer had arrived during the days following the second rice harvest of the year, before the north winds began to blow. Han Qinzai, hoisting up the placard and holding his gong, hesitated for some strange reason; like a child standing naked on the edge of the shore, about to go swimming in strange waters, he lacked the final spark of courage. In the end, even this child doesn't know at what moment and in what manner he has entered the water.

As he passed through the gate of the park and went out onto the street, he reminded himself that he must do a good job. His thoughts returned to his brief rehearsal of a few moments earlier and the deftness with which he had struck the gong. When he reached Northgate Street, he could not gauge his feeling of the moment—was it excitement or apprehension? Many of the people on the street stopped in their tracks before they even heard the sound of his gong. Han Qinzai quickly went over in his mind several times the text of his announcement: *Property tax, not propriety tax, property, property...*

The first sound of the gong accompanied his first step onto the asphalt road. But he was given a shock; with an inward shout of alarm, he quickly hugged the gong closely to his body—he didn't want any new cracks to appear because of the powerful blow he had struck the trembling gong. No one who observed the look of panic on his face could figure out what he was doing. He made a mental calculation to determine the proper force of wrist action to strike the gong again and raised the mallet high, but then his arm froze in the air—he couldn't follow through. He let his arm fall slowly and made more mental calculations. Then—bong, bong, bong—three beats of the gong that, though weak, nonetheless were loud enough to bring several people out of their houses.

> *The gong beater's coming your way—*
> *Listen everyone, here's what I have to say—*

He took a deep breath as he puzzled over why he seemed so breathless.

> *This year's property tax—*

He stopped for a moment; assuming he'd said it right, he continued:

> *And the income tax—*
> *Are due by the end of this month—*

He was extremely disappointed in the effect. This was the sort of announcing that had done him in in the first place. If you didn't put a scare into these people, who understood nothing of the importance of paying their income tax, they'd simply ignore you.

The people in this small town, seeing that the gong beater had reappeared in their midst, were brought out by their curiosity. The sight of all the people he was attracting pleased Han Qinzai as he frantically tried to think of a way to add some zip to his announcement. Then his furrowed, troubled brow went slack.

Following three beats of the gong that sounded quite satisfactory to him, he shouted out in a loud, confident voice:

> *The gong beater's coming your way—*
> *Listen everyone, here's what I have to say—*
> *This year's propriety tax and income tax—*
> *Are due by the end of the month—*
> *If it has not been paid—*
> *You know how this government office is: they'll come down on you like a chicken butcher—*

The bystanders began to laugh. Han Qinzai beat his gong three times to drown out the sounds of laughter, then went on:

> *Laugh? You can laugh after you pay your taxes—*
> *Don't you dare take any chances—*
> *If you don't believe me, see what happens when the time comes—*
> *If I, Han Qinzai, am deceiving you with my words—*
> *I, Han Qinzai, will gladly let everyone here slap my face—*

He paused. *That should do it.* In half a lifetime of beating the gong, this was the first time he had experienced a situation like the one today. No matter where he walked he had a teeming audience, and the more they laughed and carried on, the higher his spirits soared. He was secretly pleased. *Let's see the loudspeaker pedicab match this! Without me, Han Qinzai, to beat my gong, the thing wouldn't get done. I've had all I can stand of days like this. Now I'll show Scabby Head and the others how I've got it made, and I'll be surprised if they don't die of envy. I'll be able to avenge myself in my own lifetime. I'll treat them to a real feast. I'll even give them each two packs of Long Life cigarettes.*

By the time he'd passed the shops along half a block of Northgate Street, he'd made his announcement five times, and there was already a long line of curiosity seekers in his wake, all wanting to hear this comical speech a few more times. He turned his head to look at this crowd of public-spirited citizens and was given a shot in the arm by what he saw. *Just wait until I pass by the kadang tree and they witness the prestige I've gained—what'll they think then?* He had a pretty good idea what the motives of the people in his wake were, and his mind was working at full capacity: as far as he was concerned, the announcement he'd been told to make was of less importance than the embellishments he himself had added. *Oh! I know what to say now!*

A feeling of wonder and joy gushed from his heart, as three gong beats rang out in what was now practiced fashion. He said what he was supposed to say without missing a single word, although he had the feeling that he might have said "propriety" rather than "property." *But, what the hell—property, propriety, what's the difference—it's all about the same thing anyway.* Then came the important part. First three beats of the gong, then:

> *If it has not been paid—*
> *You know how this government office is: it'll come down on*
> *you like a chicken butcher—*

Hearing the roar of laughter these comments evoked, he responded with a serious warning:

> *You people may have never slaughtered a chicken, but you've*
> *seen others do it—it's no laughing matter—*

THE GONG

When the time comes, if I, Han Qinzai, have lied to you—

Bong! Bong! Bong! Three more beats of the gong.

I, Han Qinzai, will let you cut off my head and use it as a chair—

Complacently, he wiped the spittle from the corners of his mouth, feeling that this oath carried great force—how could a slap in the face compare with cutting off one's own head? Yes, that's what he'd say. How stupid he'd been in the past, believing he'd carried out his duties by merely repeating what he'd been told to say by his employer. If all along he'd done his job like he was doing it today, using his imagination to improve upon what he'd been hired to say, he'd never have fallen so low as to take himself to the kadang tree and live off coffin boards, not to mention endure all that abuse from that bunch of pigs.

The tin placard he was carrying on his shoulder, dignified though it may have been, was a lot heavier than a funeral banner. The wooden pole resting against his shoulder hurt like hell. He shifted it to his right shoulder, thereby blocking his vision to the right. When he looked off into the distance he noticed a round lacquered sign above a shop to the left with the word "wine" on it. He realized at once that this was Stony's store. His first impulse was to shift the sign back to his left shoulder, but then the self-confidence he'd so recently regained won out, for what did he have to fear now that he had his gong to beat? He didn't owe Stony too much money, and besides, Stony wasn't as heartless as Longevity. *As for Longevity, let's see what he can do now! I'll be able to pay him what I owe—I'll be a customer now!* But even with his courage pumped up, he was not totally unconcerned: his eyes never left Stony's store.

Before he'd taken but a few more steps, he was directly in front of Stony's store. Seeing Stony himself, he called out, "Stony, I'll pay you off tonight." Then, with a show of how busy he was, he turned away, even though he was frightened stiff, and beat his gong right where he was standing. He said what he'd been hired to say, then followed it with his oath. The laughter from the bystanders grew in intensity. Forcing himself to look over toward Stony, he was relieved by what he saw. Stony was certainly no Longevity: one look at his face showed you that he was a man with whom you could deal. He was thinking (actually, he was making plans, not just thinking): Crazy Cai, Taiwanese opera, good rice wine, outdoor stalls, Scabby Head and the others…. His mind was flooded with these disconnected thoughts, coming one upon the other. Sweat poured down his face until his sleeves were soaked from wiping it away. He had exerted himself to the utmost but didn't feel at all tired. He continued walking until he passed by another twenty shops or so. As he prepared to strike his gong again, a piercing screech that hung heavily in the air brought him to a stop. A dark image had darted in front of him, and he found his way blocked by a bicycle. The person on the bicycle was none other than the man from the district headquarters.

"Han Qinzai, stop at once! Go back to the district headquarters immediately!" The man had anger written all over his face, and when he finished he stepped down hard on the bicycle pedal and rode off in the direction from which he'd come.

Han Qinzai looked like a man who has sustained an electric shock; he stood there dumbly for a brief moment. Then as he watched the retreating back of the man, he yelled as loudly as he could, so that the man on the bicycle would hear him, "What's wrong? I beat the gong! Not only that, I made a special job of it!" His voice was so shrill it nearly cracked. But the man's figure was lost among the crowds on the road.

Han Qinzai felt weak all over; he turned and mumbled to the laughing people around him, "I beat it, I really did a good job. You, any one of you can bear me out on that. I beat it…" What he mumbled after this no one could say for sure. He just stood there, his head hanging down, his eyes cast to the ground. Both his left hand, which was holding the placard and his gong, and his right hand, in which he held the mallet, drooped like falling drops of water. He was soon surrounded by row upon row of curious onlookers as an atmosphere of seriousness moved outward from the center, infecting them all.

Han Qinzai listlessly took a few plodding steps forward, the crowd giving way for him. He stopped in his tracks after a few paces, raised his gong, much to the surprise of everyone, then lifted up his mallet and beat the gong loudly three times, momentarily forgetting all considerations of what he was doing. The third and final beat of the gong was muffled; a small triangular piece of brass fell to the ground. He seemed oblivious to everything as he called out in a voice tinged with madness:

> *The gong beater's coming your way—*
> *Listen everyone, here's what I have to say—*
> *This year's propriety tax and income tax—*
> *Are due by the end of the month—*

By now the sound had become a wail. He fought hard to enunciate each and every word, but it was impossible.

If by that time you don't ... you don't ...

His voice was now quivering so badly that the words were unintelligible, although his mouth continued to move as if he were still speaking. He opened and closed it with great effort. Before long there were no more sounds, but by reading his lips, the onlookers could pretty much tell that he was saying, over and over: "I, Han Qinzai... I, Han Qinzai..."

1970

Uncle Gan Geng at Dusk

One March morning, grass seeds that had fallen on the land the year before poked their heads out and, wearing quivering dewdrops on their tips, swayed in a gentle breeze.

Within a few clear, sunny days, which passed in the blink of an eye to the farmers in Guiliao-zai, most of the gravelly peanut field turned from a dull gray to a lush green after new sprouts of grass drank up the dew. The farmers, in no hurry, waited several days, until the weeds were taller than the young peanut shoots, before bringing out their rakes; everyone, young and old, set out to weed the fields.

It would take five or six days for a strapping young farmer to clear an acre of land. For a single old man, a plot this size kept him busy the year round: weeding, fertilizing, spraying insecticide, harvesting, turning the soil, and seeding. All this hard work was done with a bent back, which was why Uncle Gan Geng, now in his sixties, had developed a hump years before. He had no time to rest and no time to fret over anything; a happy smile creased his wizened face when he saw the many signs of vibrant life—harvesting, sowing the seeds, sprouting, blooming, and bearing fruit.

In only a few days, the peanut field in the village's reclaimed land by the river had been weeded and left to bake under the sun. By the following day, small mounds of dry grass piled at the edges of people's plots were set on fire. Thick, milky-white smoke, with a hint of yellow, spread the seasonal fragrance of dry grass over the fields.

Uncle Gan Geng felt a disquieting but not exactly troubling emotion. He looked up repeatedly to check the area ahead and detected the smoky fragrance of dry grass in the air. He wanted to get a sense of how many more days he'd need to clear the remaining half of his plot. Straightening up, he held the lid of his chipped clay tea jar upside down, plugged the air hole with his middle finger, and shakily filled it with enough tea for two big gulps. The sensation of fullness reminded him that he had drunk a mugful earlier. Carefully, he poured the remaining liquid back into the jar and reproached himself for being forgetful, before being reminded of the disquieting emotion a moment earlier. *As long as it doesn't rain,* he thought, *no harm will come, even if it takes me a few more days to finish. It's not going to rain, is it? It's such a clear day, so where would the rain come from?* A shivered as a cool breeze blew over. *Who knows how heaven does things?* After a momentary daze, he walked silently back to where he had been and, almost as if forced to do so, picked up his rake to loosen the gravelly soil, and then crouched down to pull out clumps of weeds. A film of fine salt crystals shimmered on his sweat-soaked black shirt, especially on the stretched spots over his arched back muscles.

As he prepared to work some more in the cool of the evening, he sensed someone standing behind him. He turned. It was a local boy whose name he could not recall. Gan Geng wasn't sure who the boy's father was, maybe Ah-song, Ah-nan, or Ah-zhang, but he knew that the boy was a grandson of Laode. He froze at the panicky look on the face of the boy, who was still panting from running hard, too breathless to speak. They stared at each other, not for long but long enough to make them both somewhat anxious; feeling a sense of urgency, they each tried to break the stifling silence.

"What's happened?"

"My—my Ah-pa told—told me to come here."

"Who's your Ah-pa?"

"Ah-nan."

"Oh—," Gan Geng said with a smile. "Then you must be Ah-hui. You and your brothers seem to have come from the same mold."

The boy nodded. "My Ah-pa is at Guangxin's shop. He told me to come tell you that your son is acting up really bad on Market Street."

Gan Geng experienced what felt like an electric shock. "So, he's out again," he muttered in a slow, thick voice. He turned to the boy. "What's he done?"

Ah-hui smiled awkwardly as he recalled the sight of Ah-xing scaring women on the street. "He's acting crazy, and he's got no clothes on." The boy forced himself to stop smiling when he noticed the old man's face twitch, as if from pain.

Tossing his rake to the ground, Gan Geng ran to the path and, oblivious to the peanut shoots he was crushing, headed for

Market Street. Ah-hui fell in silently behind him.

By the time they'd crossed two levees, passed the Earth God Temple beneath the banyan tree, and reached Niuliao, the boy had fallen behind. He couldn't help but wonder how old Uncle Gan Geng could run so far and so fast, despite his humped back. He seemed to be going even faster now. Ah-hui quickened his steps to catch up, aware that, as a boy in the fifth grade, he could not let an old man outrun him.

Once he passed Leigong Pond and emerged from its surrounding bamboo grove, Gan Geng would be on the road to Market Street, but the closer he got, the more fearful he grew. He was petrified by what might happen before he could reach his son. Ah-xing could be hurt or could hurt someone, either of which would spell trouble. He was unhappy with his aging feet for not being able to run even faster. One of the men soaking in the pond shouted when he ran past: "Uncle Gan Geng! Ah-xing is acting up, he's naked—"

"I—I've heard." He was panting so hard that no one could have heard his reply.

One of the men said to his friends loudly enough for Gan Geng to hear, "Wow! Uncle Gan Geng is in great shape. Just look at him," he said with a note of surprise, "he runs like a buffalo kicking up water; the ground shakes under his feet. See the ripples in the pond?"

They all agreed it was an apt comparison and kept their eyes on him until he disappeared into the bamboo grove. Then came Ah-hui, lumbering along with one hand on his belt.

"Are you the one who went to get Uncle Gan Geng?" they asked.

Ah-hui nodded, too breathless to speak.

"Hey—," one of the men jeered. "I'll bet he can't even blow out a candle."

Ah-yi was the first to spot Gan Geng when he shot out of the alley by Ah-yi's noodle stand. Like a paperboy peddling an extra, he shouted: "Uncle Gan Geng has arrived!"

Everyone turned to look toward the noodle stand. By the time he reached Market Street, Gan Geng was out of breath. When they saw him looking around anxiously, they all told him that his son was outside the rice mill. That is where he headed.

"Here comes Uncle Gan Geng," someone announced before he got there. "Now we'll see if you delinquents have the guts to torment Ah-xing."

Some boys stuck their heads around the corner and ran off.

"Stick around if you've got the balls," the man shouted after them. "Only cowards run away."

He turned toward Gan Geng, who was closing in. "Those wild kids are out of control," he said. "I tried to stop them, but they ignored me. Telling them to stop tormenting Ah-xing was like farting in the wind. They were throwing rocks and dirt clods at him. See, they're all over the ground."

Unable to respond, Gan Geng hurried over to his son, who cowered by a wall and tucked his head between his knees when he saw his father. With one hand on the wall and the other on his hip, Gan Geng was bent down so low his head nearly touched Ah-xing's back each time he exhaled. He could do nothing until he caught his breath, but was relieved to see that his son appeared to be unhurt. Still gasping for breath, Gan Geng wanted nothing more than to take off his shirt and wrap it around his son's waist. He turned and saw that a crowd had gathered; he heard what they were saying. It seemed they wanted him to know they cared.

"It's been a while since the last time he got out. Must have been over a year, don't you think? I recall it was the Patriarch's birthday festival."

The comment reminded the others of an amusing incident, and many of them laughed.

"But Ah-xing isn't violent, not like Shun'an's crazy uncle—" The speaker's comment was cut off before he finished.

"Ai! Shun'an's wife is scared to death of his crazy uncle. He's always grabbing women's breasts and making them run away shrieking."

"Crazy Uncle is strong, too. I hear he entered a martial arts competition at the dojo. Once his family asked some musclemen to tie him up, but he beat the hell out of them." The onlookers were getting carried away with the hot topic.

Taking his hand off the brick wall, Uncle Gan Geng straightened up to take a deep breath and finally felt the tightness in his heart ease up. But as soon as he crouched back down beside his son, the pressure surged back up, making him sigh deeply. He grabbed a handful of his son's thick black hair and yanked his head out from between his knees. When their eyes met, Gan Geng was shocked by his son's delicate features and a pale, noble expression that made him look like a martyr. Gan Geng's heart was squeezed by the pressure. Realizing that he had never been this close to his son, he studied his face carefully. A tremor ran up his spine when he looked into his son's clear eyes, which were innocent and pure, childlike even. Gan Geng felt himself shrivel up into a tiny speck and fall into those limpid pools, infused with the sensation that something had touched his soul as a void overtook his mind. All he could do was cry out with helpless sincerity and anxiety, "Heavens! Heavens!" But he was flung out of his insensate state by the incidental smile at the corners of Ah-xing's mouth. Releasing his grip on his son's hair, Gan Geng grumbled, "Haven't you done enough to torment me? Where are your clothes?"

He turned to look for them before standing up and taking off his shirt.

"Could you leave us alone?" he pleaded with the gawkers behind him.

"Get the children out of here," someone shouted.

"Yes, take them away," another joined in. "There's nothing to see here. "Come on, kids, let's go."

With their eyes still on the grownups, the children slowly stepped back and formed a circle around them.

"Why are you still here?" one of the grownups shouted. "I'm going to tell Uncle Gan Geng who threw rocks at Ah-xing. He'll break your arms and tuck them inside your bellies like slaughtered chickens."

An argument erupted among the children, who began pointing and shoving.

"You kids are terrible." Gan Geng was upset that they would pick on his son. "You're not like him, so why do you have to do that?"

When his gaze fell on one of them, the frightened boy said, "I didn't do it. It wasn't me, honest."

He looked at the boy beside him as a hint to Gan Geng.

"Well, it's good you didn't." Gan Geng was about to unbutton his shirt when Rongkun from the rice mill came out with a hempen sack and some rope.

"Here, Uncle Gan Geng, use this. You can return it tomorrow."

Gan Geng wrapped the sack around Ah-xing while the gawkers continued their animated discussion about the young man.

"How long has been it since he lost his mind?"

"I'd say ten years at least."

"Ten years?" Gan Geng said loudly as he tied the rope around his son. "Almost twenty-six years." He continued in a near whisper as if stung by that other number: "Ten years!"

"Has it been that long?"

"Of course it has. When was the Retrocession? He's been like this since he got back from the South Pacific the year after the Retrocession." Gan Geng looked helpless as he spoke in a voice drenched in sorrow. "We gave them a fine young man, and they handed him back like this, after whatever it was they did to him."

Gan Geng was having trouble tying the rope, since Ah-xing kept reaching up to tug at it. "What are you—" He couldn't bring himself to be angry with his son. "Let's go home. Don't stick around here for them to laugh at you."

"He does listen to you," someone commented.

"I'd die if he didn't, with the way he is." Gan Geng smiled bitterly, though he wasn't entirely inconsolable. "Come on, let's go home."

Ah-hui followed them silently as he recalled the first time he had ventured out to spy on Ah-xing.

Everyone on Market Street came out to watch and gossip about the pair.

"Only someone like Uncle Gan Geng would see that his crazy son is healthy and strong."

"That's life for you. Uncle Gan Geng is such a good man, but fate has not been kind to him."

"You're right. One son, and he has to be like that, and then his wife passes away."

"Heaven has no eyes!"

Gan Geng walked on and heard gossip from another group.

"It's curable, isn't it? I knew someone who was ten times worse than Ah-xing, but recovered after three months in an insane asylum."

"Don't you know, Uncle Gan Geng has tried everything. He's had a medium ask favors from the deities and a Taoist monk do magic; his wife followed a vegetarian diet at a temple; they tried both Chinese and Western medicine, even sent the boy to the Songshan Insane Asylum. Uncle Gan Geng works hard and saves everything he can, and it all goes into that bottomless pit."

"That's so sad."

What the onlookers were saying touched upon only a fraction of what he'd done, but it was all true, and they were showing either pity or admiration. Things did not seem so bad now that he had gained the respect of his neighbors by enduring the punishing hand fate had dealt him. He took in every word from the roadside. He had heard similar comments before, but none felt as comforting as they did today; that brought him so much pleasure that it wiped away most of the sadness that had been building up inside him. He felt strangely revitalized, comforted by the knowledge that he would not have done anything differently.

After a glance at the sack around his son's waist, Gan Geng reached behind Ah-xing to grab hold of the knot to prevent an awkward sight if the rope fell away in front of all these people.

"Ah-geng-zai," a grannie from Gan Geng's generation shouted shrilly, making him jerk his head around. "Your son may be crazy, but you're worse." Gan Geng was puzzled until she continued, "How could you use a hemp sack and a rope on your own son?"

Now he understood.

"Ah-xing is supposed to wear those mourning clothes for you."

The onlookers laughed.

"Ah, who cares?" he said silently. He had always been careful about signs like that, but what else could he do on this day?

"Are you a crazy old man, or aren't you? How can you have no sense of propriety?" Gan Geng's nonchalance disappointed her.

In fact, he was grateful for her kind reminder, so he smiled and said, "I'll die a happy man if he knows enough to wear mourning clothes for me, because that will mean that the old man up there is watching over us."

Startled by his unexpected reply, the old woman did not know what to do or say.

The talk of mourning reminded Gan Geng of his wife when she was about to take her last breath two years earlier. She told him to be patient with their son, no matter what. Otherwise she would not bless and protect them. "Bless and protect? What good is that? Bless and protect my ass!" he muttered.

Gan Geng continued with his earlier thoughts as they turned onto the path by Ah-yi's noodle stand. "Your mother loved you so much. You were too sick to do anything when she needed you, her only son, to wear mourning clothes and send her coffin off with an incense burner. You went so crazy, the pallbearers couldn't walk out of the house. Ai! What's the point of telling you this? People will think I'm as crazy as you."

Ah-xing was his normal silent self, walking expressionless alongside his father and looking around as if nothing were amiss. Gan Geng looked sideways at his son, as if trying to find something new. Ah-hui, in the meantime, was still quietly following them, his mind on the first time he'd gone to see Ah-xing. It had been a sweltering evening when it was impossible to sleep inside, and children from several families were playing on the threshing ground. His mother heard his sixth uncle say,

"Let's go." "Ah-hui," she said, "you're too young. I want you to stay here with Mama." Ah-hui thought back on that night, but Uncle Gan Geng's monologue was so interesting he stopped his own recollections to focus on what the old man was saying to his son.

"You—" Gan Geng paused, exhaled deeply, shook his head, and fell silent. But it didn't take him long to start up again. "Do you know how old you are?" He looked at his son.

Ah-xing still looked unaffected, walking along as carefree as could be.

"It's worse than being dead. A mute who's lost his mind. Other mutes can at least make noise, but what about you?" Gan Geng said with no rancor, looking helpless. "Of course you don't know your age. You're forty-six! Some of the lucky ones have grandchildren at forty-six. Forty-six!" Gan Geng turned to look at Ah-xing before his voice took on a more serious tone. "You're forty-six, Ah-xing," he said, as if his son had a working mind. After a while he spoke up again, sounding more like he was supplying an answer for his son. "Forty-six is forty-six, but it will be the same at sixty-four." Gan Geng smiled. "It's true. What are you smiling at?" He reproached himself. "I know. I was just saying." He smiled again. "You don't know who I am, do you?" He looked down, seemingly seeing nothing or wanting to see anything.

Ah-hui, who was still walking behind them, did not know what to make of the prolonged silence. Uncle Gan Geng grunted and took a leisurely glance at Ah-xing, who remained miles away from everything around him. A touch of sadness flitted across the old man's heart, and he said, "Who am I?" He paused. "Look familiar, don't I?" The hint of a smile froze on his face. "You have absolutely no idea who I am."

He was reminded of the time a month earlier when Ah-xing

had smashed a toilet to pieces, splattering the floor and walls with urine and excrement. Gan Geng had been so flustered he couldn't bring himself to clean the place up. Finally he pulled himself together and got to work, but within an instant, Ah-xing was out of sight. Gan Geng wondered where he'd gone to wreak more havoc before he'd even had time to clean up the mess. Distressed and irritated, he ran all around the house, shouting himself hoarse for his son. In the end he found him on the bamboo bridge. He was standing in the middle of it, shaking the railing so violently that the bridge would have fallen into the water, taking Ah-xing with it, if his father hadn't reached him in time. Gan Geng rushed up to his son with his fists raised, but instead of hitting him, the blows fell heavily on his own bony chest. Spurred by the pain, he beat himself until he was crying over the bitterness of his fate. Ah-xing, on the other hand, stood to the side as if alone, as if nothing had happened. "You have absolutely no idea who I am." Gan Geng felt a dull ache in his chest when he recalled that day. "You should at least know that I'm your slave, someone who still cleans you up even now."

His hand felt weak and was trembling, but he tightened his grip on the knot as he gently pushed Ah-xing ahead. Gan Geng knew he would never get an answer from his son. It was all one-sided speculation bordering on self-mockery; since it was impossible to get through to his son, he turned it into a burning desire for self-exploration. That was a new experience for him, and not so surprisingly, it took the form of pretending to be someone else asking questions. He thought about his age. *Ai! How did I manage to make it through these years? I'm sixty-seven or sixty-eight, more likely older, I'm sure.* He turned again to glance at Ah-xing, who was mumbling something. *That's my son, Ah-xing.* With his eyes fixed on his son, the enigmatic expression on his face gave way to a look of pain. He longed for Ah-xing to listen to him at that moment, as if he'd lost touch with reality.

"Do you remember, Ah-xing?" He turned to look at the road ahead. "You and I once wanted to plant something on the sandbar downstream, but Zaitian and his family are using it now. It was over a thousand square feet, and they're able to harvest peanuts one season and sweet potatoes the next. They laugh twice a year, their mouths gaping from ear to ear—"

"My stomach hurt so much, I thought I'd die before you came back. People said I should have it checked, but I didn't. I knew there had to be a big hole in there and that the doctor would want to operate. It would be very hard, since we didn't have any money and you weren't home to help out.

"I thought everything would change for the better when you came back. Who could predict that you would return like this? You would not have known where we lived if I hadn't gone to meet you at Keelung Harbor. But what was strange was that my problem stomach slowly improved once you were home, until it stopped hurting altogether. I have to say the heavens did not stop watching over the Gan family then. There's no other explanation for it." By this time they were walking on the floodplain between the levees. "The water level has fallen lately and created sandbars. The families in Guiliao-zai divided up the sandbars, and every family got to plant something, everyone but us. Because of you, we had to give up our share."

Gan Geng went on and on, saying whatever came to mind and talking about everything he saw, not caring whether Ah-xing was listening or not. At some point, however, he turned quiet. They'd covered some distance in silence by the time Ah-hui realized that the old man had stopped talking. Uncle Gan Geng seemed the same, though, with a severely humped back, his head hanging low, like a wild animal keeping its nose to the ground to sniff out its prey. He plowed through the heavy air of the descending dusk, his hand securely on the knot and resting on Ah-xing's hip, turning it into an extension of the young man. Watching father and son from behind, Ah-hui retraced the thread of his recollection and thought back to the first time he had seen Ah-xing and how frightened he'd been.

It was a sultry night, too hot to sleep inside and not a breeze outside. Ah-hui, who was about as tall as the early rice sprouts, was following closely behind his sixth uncle and some other older boys as they took a shortcut through the rice paddies, something they would never have dared to do in broad daylight. The grownups would have given them a good beating if they had seen the boys knocking kernels off the stalks. Soon they were ducking under the bamboo fence at Uncle Gan Geng's house. Like scouts checking out enemy territory, the eight boys sneaked to the back of the house, where they spotted a prison-like room by the cow pen. One side of the room was the mud wall of the house, while the other three sides were made of thick bamboo poles more than a meter tall. Tree branches the size of the bamboo poles filled in the gaps.

On such a dark night they could not see anything without getting close, so they inched nearer and nearer until they all had their hands on the bamboo poles, with their faces sticking through the gaps. Finally they saw everything. It was deadly quiet; the only sound came from cows swishing their tails and stamping their hooves. Ah-xing was sitting on a simple bed, casting an oversized shadow before the boys. They watched, not knowing what else to do, when Ah-xing abruptly started to shout orders to Japanese soldiers: "Attention!" "At ease!" The boys had often heard him do this, either at home or as they walked by, but this was the first time they had been this close to his shouts, especially Ah-hui, who had never been there before. When the first shout burst from Ah-xing's lips, the boys were so scared they turned to run away. But Ah-hui's head was stuck between two poles. Gazing at Ah-xing's back now, the memory still gave him a scare, though he laughed it off.

At that moment, Uncle Gan Geng switched the knot to his other hand and spotted Ah-hui when he moved to walk to Ah-xing's other side. "Ah-hui," Uncle Gan Geng called out for no obvious reason before turning back to the road after giving the boy a brief smile. After only a few steps, he strained to look back at the boy. "Ah-hui." Uncle Gan Geng wore a worry-free smile. "Do you remember how you fell ill after being frightened by Ah-xing when you were four or five?" Ah-hui was still recovering from the scare brought on by his memory when Uncle Gan Geng mentioned the same incident. Surprised by the coincidence, the boy could only stare blankly.

Walking sideways was too much for the old man, so he turned and walked backward to talk to the boy, like a plow being pulled along. "Your mother came to ask for some of Ah-xing's hair," Uncle Gan Geng said. "She soaked some of it in bathwater to rub all over you and then braided what was left in red thread for you to wear. You got better." Uncle Gan Geng laughed. "You don't remember? You must have forgotten. It was a long, long time ago." He looked back at his son. "And Ah-xing has no idea what happened."

His voice was so faint the boy could not hear him.

"Come over here, Ah-hui." Uncle Gan Geng pointed to a spot

nest to him. Ah-hui quietly walked up to the old man. Uncle Gan Geng tilted his head slightly to look at him. "Ah-xing could read, just like you. That was before we had a school in Guangxing, so he had to go study on Market Street. Back then he crossed the river with your father and the other boys before it was light out. He had excellent penmanship and often received three red circles on his notebook from his teacher." Uncle Gan Geng glanced at the boy again. "How many red circles do you get?"

"None."

"None?" The old man was incredulous. "Not even one?" He turned to look at the boy.

"We don't do red circles."

"Then what do you do?"

"Our teachers give us ABCs."

"Oh! A is the best, then."

"A+."

"Then the three red circles Ah-xing got would be A+." The old man recalled the time Ah-xing had opened his notebook to show him the three red circles and asked for some coins. "Good boy! You did the work and you got three red circles."

Ah-hui wasn't quite sure what Uncle Gan Geng meant, but he didn't dare ask him.

"Have you gone to catch crabs in the river, Ah-hui?"

"No." The boy paused before adding, "I've never seen any there."

They were still walking on the floodplain between the levees.

"That's true. There aren't any now. There isn't a drop of water in the river, so how would we see crabs?" the old man said emotionally. "It wasn't like this in the old days, when the water ran in torrents. When Ah-xing passed by on his way home after school, he could simply overturn a few rocks and come home with a string of crabs. Especially in the winter you'd open the shell and see every crab filled with roe, which we ate until our lips were yellow; we even shit yellow oil. I really don't know where all the crabs have gone."

"My papa has caught crabs, too."

Uncle Gan Geng didn't seem to hear the boy. The three of them quietly walked along, trailed by the crisp sounds of shifting pebbles.

"Ah-xing, don't ever cross the Toutiao River by yourself; make sure to find someone to do it with you."

The boy thought that the warning was directed at him. But why had Uncle Gan Geng called him Ah-xing? He looked up at the old man.

"The Toutiao River is a terrible spot. In the old days, Muyang and Yongyu both lost a child to the river, and some of the elementary school students who came from Market Street to hike here were also carried away by the water."

"My papa told me that. But there's hardly any water in the river now."

"That's true. What I meant was, be careful later when the water returns.

"The Japanese back then were foolhardy; they didn't believe in gods or ghosts. We wanted to put on a play by the river, but they wouldn't allow it no matter what we said," Uncle Gan Geng continued. "Ah-xing, if a play is put on to chase away evil spirits, it will start with a black-faced figure jumping onto the stage. Little kids shouldn't watch that part. If you happen to see it, you must quickly pluck a green leaf and put it in your mouth, and then you'll be fine. Little kids can't be foolhardy."

Ah-hui realized that Uncle Gan Geng had called him Ah-xing

again. He looked at the old man, who was walking with his head down, and said, "My mama said the same thing."

Silence returned. The sounds of shifting pebbles disappeared once they reached the levee, where the old man took a short break. He looked back at his peanut field, his house, and the enormous setting sun above the roof.

They slid down to the other side of the levee after standing there for a while, as the sun leaped onto the tips of the chinaberry tree by the house. They started walking again, in silence. The sun rolled from the tip of the tree to its trunk, looking even bigger than before, as if they were getting closer.

"Ah-xing. I mean, Ah-hui."

The old man laughed when he realized he'd called the boy by the wrong name. "Would you run over to my peanut field and get my rake and the tea jar?"

"Sure," the boy said, and took off running.

"Watch out for the peanut sprouts, Ah-hui!" Uncle Gan Geng called out.

He took the opportunity to switch the hand holding the knot and exhaled after another look at his on. "Your mother told me to take you out for a walk around the field every evening." He sounded apologetic. "But you see, where would I find the time to do that? Everyone else has weeded their peanut field. I still have a third of it left." A smile emerged on his face when he imagined the vibrant signs of life on the lush green peanut shoots as they reached up and quivered in the breeze. "I think we'll have more peanuts this year."

The sun had landed on the horizon, where it burned open a fiery bright spot, reducing everything in front of it to dark outlines, like figures in a puppet show. From a distance, Ah-hui could see the dark shadows of their backs as he returned with the rake and the tea jar. By the time he jumped onto the path to catch up with them, however, he was directly facing the setting sun, and the moving shadows seemed to tumble into the dazzling opening on the horizon. He frowned, holding up the jar to block the light, but failed to see father and son; he nearly cried out in panic.

It got dark quickly. In the sky above the village, a scant few stars appeared, trickling down a faint glow. At that moment everyone in the village could hear Uncle Gan Geng wielding his hammer to pound a long nail into the bamboo pole that bolted the gate on Ah-xing's enclosure. Amid the sounds of pounding, the young man's intermittent shouts of "Kiotsuke!" and "Yasumei!" were carried on the evening air, sending a chill into everyone's heart.

1971

www.ingramcontent.com/pod-product-compliance
Lightning Source LLC
Chambersburg PA
CBHW021432080526
44588CB00009B/506